Praise for *The Anger M...*

Walter Polt's invitation to turn typical anger into healthy power invites a very deep consideration of how we are able to be powerful, self-compassionate, loving and clear. This is a book we all need and a book that will offer helping professionals an active and proven methodology to help clients . . . It gives us all tools that will be useful in communicating with others *and* in working through issues within ourselves to become authentic and true to our deepest Selves. I highly recommend this book!
— Dorothy Firman, EdD, USA
Director, The Synthesis Center
Editor, *The Call of Self: Psychosynthesis Life Coaching*

This is a clear, wise and very instructive manual for turning your anger into your powerful ally. The transmutation of the combative energies causing so much conflict in the world was a central theme for Roberto Assagioli, the father of Psychosynthesis. I recommend this book wholeheartedly .
— Kenneth Sørensen, Denmark
Former Director of Training,
Norwegian Institute of Psychosynthesis
Author of *The Soul of Psychosynthesis*

Walter Polt has taken on a crucial human emotion—anger—in all its varieties ranging from protective/healthy to self-destructive/harmful. The difference makes all the difference. Let Walter inform you and guide you in how best to live with this most universal of feelings.
— Richard Schaub, PhD, USA
Director, Huntington Meditation and Imagery Center
Co-Author of *Transpersonal Development*

This book is a true gift. It offers a simple, practical, yet very powerful tool, and I gladly recommend it to all my colleagues and all those who are engaged in a process of personal development.
— Petra Guggisberg Nocelli, Switzerland
Author of *The Way of Psychosynthesis*

Walter's book works. Whether our anger spits and simmers, or whether it shoots out like a rocket, it often doesn't do anything except create more anger. He shows us how to turn it around and use the energy for good. I use it, I appreciate it, and I recommend it.
— Jan Kuniholm, USA
Founding Editor, *Psychosynthesis Quarterly*

More Praise for *The Anger Makeover*:

Walter Polt has created a very practical workbook that will be invaluable for anyone with anger issues, presenting an effective approach to the 'management' of anger, not through denial, repression or acting out but through looking within to find the power locked behind the emotional response. An excellent book on the subject.
— Will Parfitt, England, UK
Psychosynthesis Teacher and Trainer
Author of *Psychosynthesis: The Elements and Beyond*

Many years ago, the original Anger-Makeover process, then called the Anger-to-Power process, helped me to see both anger and power in a positive light. Seeing anger as a reflection of my values was a key to becoming less judgmental of self and others. Walter Polt's updated edition, *The Anger Makeover*, sheds more of this positive light with its many detailed and easily understood explanations, grounded in modern neuroscience.
— Douglas Russell, USA
Founder and Editor, *Psychosynthesis Digest*

Anger remains a powerful human expression, which unfortunately often negatively affects us and our relationships. Polt's *Anger Makeover* process helps us transform the often-negative aspects of raw anger into a constructive resource for growth and healing. A proven practical guide!
— Ilene Val-Essen, PhD, USA
Author of *Bring Out the Best in Your Child and Yourself*

Walter Polt has given the world and the fortunate readers of this book a rare gem. *The Anger Makeover* is thorough, descriptive and clear in its exposition of Polt's insightful, yet simple-to-apply, transformative process. I know—because I immediately put Polt's process to work, both personally and with clients, with amazing results!
— Barbara Veale Smith, MEd, USA
Founder of *The Undefended Heart.org*
Board Certified Psychosynthesis Coach

In this fine book Polt takes anger, something usually in malevolent clothing, and puts it into a different outfit. We want the energy that's there in anger, yet we're wary of doing harm. Over and over again, he shows us how, if we can slow down and take a moment, we can use the energy without inflicting the harm. It's especially helpful when the book addresses people who don't usually speak up for themselves.
— Ron Seybold, USA
Author of *Viral Times* and *Stealing Home*

THE ANGER MAKEOVER

DISCOVER YOUR POWER TO
REFORM YOUR RELATIONSHIPS

WALTER POLT

CHESHIRE CAT BOOKS

Published by
Cheshire Cat Books

P.O. Box 599
Cheshire, MA 01225-0599 USA
www.Cheshire-Cat-Books.com

Cover by Asya Blue www.asyablue.com

The material in this book is intended for educational purposes
only. No expressed or implied warranty is given or liability taken
as to the use of this material. Users of this book are advised to
seek professional assistance, guidance or support should they
encounter any difficulty in applying the material herein.

ISBN 978-0-9882024-3-6

Library of Congress Control Number: 2021947574

ACKNOWLEDGMENTS

I am deeply grateful to Jan Kuniholm for his vision in encouraging me to create this new edition and helping to get it published. Dr. Richard Schaub has been extremely helpful. I owe much to many people for helping the original book and this revision to become published realities. Cynthia Lashley, PhD, my wife, is so good at keeping visions alive. Her sense of urgency and timeliness have helped me keep my own faith going, through setbacks and fleeting years. Her brilliant energy and her quickness and skill with words have helped my writing tone become more immediate and real. Her editing has helped bring out the depth and power of this *Anger-Makeover* process and bring order to my creative chaos. My sister, Sister Cecilia Polt, OSB, graciously allowed me to write the original drafts of this book to her in the form of letters even when she was traveling the world from Nebraska to Namibia to Tanzania. She was most receptive and offered invaluable editing suggestions as well as samples of how she used the process. My wordsmith friend Pat Sauer helped me add sparkle and insight. My dear niece Anita Polt gave invaluable suggestions from an awakened layperson's perspective.

Many professionals have encouraged this book. Molly Young Brown worked with this process in our training work together and included me and what was then called the Anger-to-Power process in her *Growing Whole* books. She and other therapists such as Dr. Phyllis Clay, Dr. Jack Schooley, and Katie Fashing reminded me over the years of how useful and powerful the process is and of how they continued to use it in their personal and professional lives.

Doug Russell first published the article "From Anger to Power" in the *Psychosynthesis Digest* in 1984. Andre and Paul Pare translated the *Digest* article into French as *De la colère au pouvoir*, and the *Centre de integration de la personne de Quebec Inc.* published the French translation as a monograph in its "*Intégration*" series in 1992, making it available to a larger audience.

Stanley Hadsell, with whom I spent many hours writing

about this process and discussing how to present it, gave many insights about how the process has been used in a hospital setting and with groups.

This book got 100% better after Ron Seybold became its editor. His masterful hand made my writing feel stronger and simpler to me. It has fewer and better words and punctuation marks, and I benefited from his encouragement and wise suggestions, including advising me of Asya Blue's brilliance designing book covers and interiors. As you can see, he was right.

I thank the many friends who have discussed these ideas with me and encouraged my work. Finally, numerous clients have used this process, expanded on it, and helped me become more precise in applying it. I am grateful to all.

Walter J. Polt
August 2021

CONTENTS

PREFACE

This book is a revision of *From Anger to Power,* which I published in 1996. It has a lot of the same content, but it's clearer and easier to use and bolstered by brain science revelations and my growing awareness of our nonjudgmental spiritual oneness. Its new title, *The Anger Makeover,* suggests that I'm not espousing "power over." Also, this edition zeroes in on relationship conflicts. It's about ordinary anger with people we have strong ties to: life partners, friends, and colleagues. We need conflicts. They're part of life. But they must make things better, not worse. To make this happen for you, it's easiest to start with conflicts that occur at work or at home. It's a new tone, not forcing anyone—but yes, sometimes satisfying everyone.

Effective conflict, by definition, makes things better. To get on board with this, I recommend starting in everyday life with coworkers, friends, and loved ones. Effective conflicts only happen in a context of friendship and respect; otherwise they're ineffective or destructive conflicts. That's why I'm suggesting we first attend to the conflicts in our good relationships. With those, we have reason to hope we can keep friendship and respect foremost throughout. With a colleague or loved one, we usually trust that there is no harmful intent. Even with colleagues and friends, if the conflict is about politics or any intense moral conviction, it can be hard to keep that trust afloat. Knowing that doesn't make that trust easier for you. The psychology of intense convictions is vast and ongoing. When you consider the conundrum of someone in some far-away place having a moral reaction equal to yours, but about a "truth" opposite yours, you see why I'm limiting my focus in this book to day-to-day knee-jerk issues within close relationships.

In this book I ask you to practice on a single conflict you're in the middle of or can see coming. You'll learn the Anger-Makeover process much faster. And again, you may want to choose something not related to politics. In politics, at least those on TV, we don't have many good models. We don't see many conflicts that preserve friendship. Both sides trash each other, accuse each other, and use abuse and scare tactics. Political discussions today can get hard and nasty fast. They become standoffs, even between people who have a relationship. Nastiness does something, but not what a positive vision does. Blaming is easy, almost automatic, but not helpful. And at home and work, it will invite hurt and anger but not move your partner. Personally, when I feel someone dissing me, I'm not convinced of anything, and I certainly don't feel closer. If we want movement, progress, and synthesis, we need to experience our feelings but learn to find the positive intentions on both sides. Without this, the irritation ratchets up.

I suggest readers start their Anger-Makeover practice sessions by putting big issues on the shelf and focusing on everyday situations. Breakthroughs come from repeated small restructurings of our brains' old, habitual pathways. While these breakthroughs are not easy, they are joyful events. That kind of joy makes our practicing productive. Just reading this book is not enough. You must get started right away practicing and feeling your personal power, again and again.

As we go along practicing—again, it does take practice—we start to remember that for richer relationships we don't need to convince. We need to differentiate, to respect and appreciate how we're different. We don't need to erase differences. We can't. We are different. Fortunately, as we shall see, we can often with care and time combine differences—even opposite values.

Relationship synthesis is new territory for many people. And what makes it so challenging is that conflicts switch our primitive, reptilian, flight-fight-freeze-fawn brain mechanisms to "on," and at the same time they turn our loving, nonjudgmental Self to "off." That slows down conflict resolution. We will find out how to continually bring ourselves back to unconditional love by being nonjudgmental, behaving always with kindness, and staying curious. That means not just loving the loved one who is challenging us. It starts with loving ourselves—replacing doubts, regrets, and self-anger with self-healing, vision, and constructive thinking. That may be as hard as squeezing through a slender passageway, but it leads to a whole new world. It means developing a habit of twofold consciousness when a conflict arises. We must not simply be in the nonjudgmental spirit that we are part of. We must also hold close and gain wisdom from the rambunctious, judgmental, angry, and passionate powerhouse that is part of us. When in conflict, we need both energies: the wisdom in our spirit, and the wisdom waiting inside our anger.

For years now, brain-activity imaging has been giving us more and more information. Lots of helpful studies show how our brains jump into "fight or flight" mode. This happens not just in truly traumatic situations, but also in ones that only seem traumatic. If you learn to stay alert in your relationships with coworkers and loved ones, you start noticing when that survival reflex is happening. If you stand back from it, you realize it's constantly happening mistakenly with relatively small, day-to-day annoyances and irritations. In other words—and this is all natural—when we are startled in this day-to-day world, our brains' old programing is still repeatedly getting things wrong. Quick predictions during catastrophes got your prehistoric ancestors and mine through eons of threatening situations in the wild. How come we were the lucky survivors? Our brains learned to sound an alarm instantly, even for possible danger. Notice: at the same time that survival instincts are important, they're a huge hazard to civilization's survival. As psychiatrist-scientist-trainer Daniel Siegel (2011) points out, "When our entire focus is on self-defense, no matter what we do . . . we can't open ourselves enough to hear our partner's words accurately" (p. 214). Even in close relationships, our survival instincts lock us in combat.

The personal-survival part has worked because our brain, without asking any permission, still continues to overcompensate. But this may be our undoing. We may not survive as a species, because the neural combat machinery misleads us into harsh judgments. And again notice: It then keeps us misled. Once we judge a person, it can seem impossible to un-judge them. And in these uncivilized times, this judgment is often much ado about saving our self-image, or showing we are right, or trying to guard our carefully cultivated picture of how things should be. We even wish we could force our righteous picture on someone else.

That's why in conflicts with colleagues or family, we get distracted. The first place to look is not at what the partner just said or did, but at the reaction happening inside us. The point is not to turn off the brain's alarm bell. That may take some minutes. We just have to watch and listen while it is ringing, feel where it registers in our body, and smile at it with appreciation. Then we must check it for important safety information. It's seldom a safety problem. Usually it's all about an inner preference or value needing attention, something in us we need to embrace.

The examples in this book are from real life, though some are composites of several people's experience. Identities have been radically changed so any similarity to persons living or dead is coincidental. The exceptions are friends who gave permission to use their names.

This book is not a substitute for training or therapy. It is for information, enjoyment, and personal and spiritual growth. If you need additional guidance or therapeutic assistance, I encourage you to seek the help of a competent professional.

And whether or not you are a professional therapist or coach, you bear full responsibility, and get all credit, for your results using the information and exercises in this book.

INTRODUCTION

This book helps you turn your old opinion about anger inside out, so you can see anger's better outcomes. You'll learn that anger is a tricky energy with positive potential. I will guide you to an inward enjoyment of the energy underneath anger. That's a very different feeling, because it lives in another place in your brain— the heart of your unique power and values. The process described here is a big step toward effective outward self-expression. This book will ready you for new goals: ultimately, to connect your reserved abilities, such as curiosity and listening, with your expressive skills, such as gentle talk and gestures. It will prepare you to help resolve problems, first with people close to you, and eventually with others not so close.

Respectful, successful conflict is central to human development and to improving relationships. I describe five practical steps that reduce the often-hidden tension left behind an anger episode. Reducing this tension can enrich close relationships. These five steps are for ordinary anger. But they don't shut it down. We need to gain the positive energy buried in it, to pull out warm, powerful energy and put it to use, to transform discomfort into satisfaction and relief.

I recently woke from a dream hearing the question, "What is the principal principle?" It's this: When someone you love bugs you or shocks you, you can transform your hot-tempered energy to enjoy relief and harmonious growth. That's important, because when you're annoyed, neuroscience now tells us that the instinctual, reptilian part of your brain doesn't just sound an alarm; it also shoves wrong information and snap judgments into your thinking. One man I worked with said, "This book opened up a way to a deeper, stronger, wiser part of my being."

A psychologist and author I admire told me "this book addresses the tricky task of bringing something instinctual and automatic into consciousness and choice. This information can literally change lives, so it is very important." Our built-in instinctual triggers fool us, even in a loving relationship. They keep on trying to fool me. My inner reactions to an offense can be everything from ruffled feathers to full battle mode, and either of these can leave one bitter and guarded. We all need skills to transform each anger event, and further, we need to continue using the skills to develop a new habit. Even the Dalai Lama, to his eternal credit, said, in a speech at the University of New Mexico, "I have to work at this every day myself."

This Book's Promise

We've all had someone close to us judge us and try to fix us or correct our errors, and we wanted to do the same right back. Are such dialog-jams inevitable in loving relationships? Yes, so it's important to correct the misinformation our alarm bell reactions leave with us. We can transform the irritation by paying attention to those sparks of anger—and questioning the beliefs left behind. We're guided to step away from the knee-jerk reaction, which is thoughtless and often destructive, see it up close, and use its energy to move forward to a heartfelt response by identifying with the more powerful positive energy hidden there. I promise: Each time anger flares up, you can benefit. Together, we will deliver on this promise every time you use the five easy steps I describe here.

Brain Science Update

Developments in neuroscience have boomed since the first edition of this book. They dramatically lit up my understanding of day-to-day resentments. We humans spent eons straining to stay alive in the wild, and to this day, harsh judgments accompany our reflexes. "It's an attack! It's an enemy!" Even as our inner alarms jolt us, they fool us. When we feel offended or attacked, a twisted picture gets stamped across our thinking. By habitually using the five steps in this book, we can repeatedly correct that picture—and salvage much-needed energy.

Trekking to Inner Wisdom

Thanks to my stops and stumbles along the way, I developed this now well-used process. I benefited from great teachers and writers—and I searched my own heart. The process delivers life-changing suggestions that square with my own experience. Let me share bits of my long trek. It will encourage you to expand your vision.

In the culture I grew up in, religion was everything—but it wasn't explicit about resolving human squabbles. Yes, "love everybody" is vital, but we need specifics about putting that into practice. And I don't think we can love everybody if we keep eternal punishment in the picture as a threat. Terror is not helpful.

Schools have taught wonderful things, but educators seem not to know how important it is to make conflict respectful and healthy. To them, the central challenge must have seemed impossible: how to define differences as something natural, plus how to turn conflict exchanges into something loving and peaceful. And schools were even worse for a friend of mine. He said, "In my schools, unhealthy conflict was the rule. And it was ubiquitous. I think it was unconsciously encouraged."

Grad School: Learning to Listen

During my graduate work at Columbia University, the best thing I learned from top-notch teachers and writers was how to listen. Listening with unconditional positive regard was magic—essential growth for me. And it was great to learn to help folks with disorders. But I was more interested in helping typical people without disorders toward robust living. I longed to offer clients practical tools with easy-to-grab handles. People everywhere who are already essentially healthy need to relieve frustrations with loved ones, get past roadblocks, and become more alive. And a big question that never got answered was, "What can regular, flawed, harassed humans like me do with our anger?"

A Larger Landscape

I got real answers from two effective leaders. They changed my life. One was Roberto Assagioli, a neurologist and psychiatrist. In 1910 in Florence, Italy, he began developing an approach to growth called Psychosynthesis. The other leader was a student of Assagioli's. Dr. Edith Stauffer, that silver-haired dynamo, redefined forgiveness not as weakness, but as what I would call "good-will with bones." Here, suddenly, was a new lay of the land.

Psychosynthesis combined psychology and spirit. It showed me how to step back from the variety of players inside myself and work with them respectfully and lovingly. I stopped judging rowdy parts of me. I stopped trying to get rid of them. It also boosted my interest in peaceful conflict. I learned that even people's knee-jerk reactions came from specialized parts inside them focused on an important detail. Instinctual reactions were specifically dedicated to correcting something, with the intent of achieving a specific goal. Suddenly the objective during fight-or-flight survival moments became a new one: to honor the needs and capabilities of these internal parts—and to have them shed light on the solution. You could then embrace these reactions in a new synthesis.

Stauffer's work, built on Assagioli's, further enlarged my anger-management toolbox. In an Unconditional Love and Forgiveness workshop in the early 1970s in rural New Hampshire, she taught how to spot the demands in your anger and change them into simple affirmations of your preferences—and still reaffirm your continued love. Another synthesis: preferences and open appreciation. And this work was not just to help the other person. It would help you, by releasing conditions, restrictions on your natural, divine love and friendship.

Teach These Anger-Altering Tools to Groups?

I found Psychosynthesis and Stauffer's teachings on how to highlight preferences effective—and good for mutual respect. I saw individuals and couples improving their lives and getting dramatic tension relief. I thought, "I could easily teach fellow professionals how to use these tools."

I did teach it. And the workshops were magical—for people like me. Growing up with two older, bigger, tougher brothers, I had more practice developing my reserved, self-control skills in conflicts than my expressive skills. As a consequence, in my workshops I didn't grasp that participants, and I myself, also needed to be reminded of something important: that even when we think it's hopeless to voice our perspectives, we need to work at learning to voice them. In my workshops, the participants who learned to transform their anger into useful energy were the more-reserved folks. They were more alive and capable when they completed the workshops.

However, I needed to offer a bigger picture, one that didn't only include the "be reserved" worldview. A participant woke me up to this after a workshop where I had asked a roomful of people to say loudly and in unison, "I'm angry!" Indeed, that was the energy most of these participants needed to get more in touch with—but this particular participant was already in touch with her anger. She needed help controlling her expressive side. She was concerned, and rightly so. "Now I'm worked up," she said. "What do I do?" Answering that tough question became part of the Anger Makeover. As a result, now you can use this process to combine those urgent, opposite instincts of fight and flight. This book prepares us to respond with reserve, but not be too reserved. We can also respond with expression, but only the expression appropriate to each situation.

So let's begin to increase your respect for your anger—and start turning it inside-out to see its bigger, better options. The energy in your anger is just waiting for your guidance.

PART I

Anger, Power,
and
A Process for Finding Power

Anger

In Relationship Conflicts

Anger May Feel Like Power.
It Is, When Shifted to the Positive.

Anger is a Pathway to Self

Anger can lead you to inner power—regularly. We do not have to keep blindly buying into knee-jerk reactions and stay stuck in low-level fight-or-flight mode.

Edward Viljoen wrote the striking and very practical book *Ordinary Goodness* (2017), a text totally devoted to day-to-day transformation. His courageous and unwavering vision complements my Anger-Makeover process. In describing this knee-jerk problem and its lasting false impressions, he cited the high cost of being "hooked on a feeling." He recounted (p. 24) how "repeatedly fear, anger, jealousy, desire, love and the like had . . . the authority to control [his] actions" in his stead. He wasn't asking himself what was the right thing to do.

What do we know about our triggers, reactions, impulses? They're vital in a crisis, but there's a lesson we absolutely must learn again in every generation. In most conflicts, we must back out of our own impulses to check them. And then we must neutralize their clingy aftereffects. That's hard, because the ordinary impulsive moment is a hormone bath. Our brain flips into a prehistoric pattern.

And it's an addictive one; we love it. In a moment of anger there are brain regions and functions that get turned on that might be called our pleasure center. In a webinar, Joan Borysenko, PhD, author of *Minding the Body, Mending the Mind*, was just one of the experts discussing this irony. (To encourage readers to explore the term, "pleasure center" is short for a complicated range of brain parts and hormones and electrical connections involved in sweetening beneficial but difficult experiences, one being the emotion of anger.)

Anger all by itself would be an extremely difficult experience. Yet we need anger to survive. Sometimes, in a real crisis, raw anger reactions are necessary. But we could never face such hard actions as combat or running away from combat if our brain hadn't learned to sugarcoat the grim impulse. If anger was not exciting, we'd all have failed to survive. Evolution made sure we would. It made anger pleasurable. And there's another way we've evolved. The reflex-reptile part of our brain takes over by making things simple. It pushes its agenda while shutting off our brain's thinking and empathy.

Now we know this is a design flaw. It leaves the lizard brain isolated. Although we have evolved generosity and empathy and thoughtfulness too, those abilities are routinely blocked and forgotten. Anger much too regularly and dramatically seizes instantaneous control. Anger is all that's available, and we buy in to it. It feels so logical and right. When we wake up to what happened, we know the impulse just did an end run around logic. And so it's seldom logical and right. The issue is not survival after all. This flaw has put us in a bind. Early humans survived by doing anger on autopilot. That loss of empathy and thought is now exactly what is jeopardizing our survival. As we continue our default, fight, flee, blame, shame, and so on, our survival chances as a species keep getting slimmer. If we don't learn to pause and question the wisdom of each raw-anger incident, we may soon not be here at all. Almost every raw-anger impulse needs alteration. We're not going to be able to change our primeval, set training until we catch on to the fact that our impulses, even around the house and at the office, are usually distorted. Like a bad diet, they are a little too enjoyable. They are so closely connected to our pleasure centers that even in day-to-day angry moments we don't want to change. It's even hard to simply consider changing. We're presented with a challenge: to form new habits. That's why I offer this book. You'll see me coming back to this throughout the book and from different angles. We can and must practice monitoring and revising our frustration impulses.

Luckily, we can put our impulsive, too sweet, knee-jerk impatience to good use. That's this book's good news, and it comes just in the nick of time. Our chronic anger-tension lifestyle has been working against us and our world so long that these days we see people acting as if being impulsive and nasty is perfectly acceptable, as if their words and actions don't make things worse, or even lead to division, violence, and destruction.

What's worse, when others are in their knee-jerk mode, your brain may snap into its own knee-jerk mode—and yours may be an even bigger one. To my always-ready hothead mode, anyone else's hothead mode looks unsafe, so my hothead mode instantly clicks on. Either we learn new habits and a new lifestyle, and practice, establish, and model the new pattern whenever we can, or we're dead. Fortunately, once we've firmly decided to escape the old pattern, we have simple, very effective tools to change our lifestyle. The clear steps of the Anger-Makeover process help create a new reality, and it's lovely that we can start with people close to us.

Pushy Me and Timid Me

It surely is true that in any conflict, when we are favoring our expressive, pushy, angry side (and maybe showing poor impulse control) we may trigger reactions we don't want, ranging from nasty feelings to violence. Yet when we are favoring our mild-mannered side, it doesn't always help matters to retreat into silence. Am I suggesting that if we're a person that's usually mild-mannered we should monitor our impulses less? Of course not. The first thing we all need to do when an angry impulse hits us is pause. And during the pause, we can do what Resmaa Menakem teaches in his book *My Grandmother's Hands* (2017): carefully sense what's happening in our bodies and take time to feel and finally start to metabolize the pain our bodies have inherited and stored. For centuries, our ancestors have felt and watched untold traumas, disappointments, and mistreatment.

Once we have started this monitoring and settling of our body's process by feeling what it's feeling, we can use the Anger-Makeover steps in this book to direct the process. We will move into new territory, exploring our personal preferences and values. We will enjoy standing where we stand and determining what's important to us in the present encounter. We need to do this not just at times when we feel expressive, but also when we're being more mild-mannered or too shy. In that way, our response will come from a more settled body and stable heart.

Often a precious insight emerges that makes it clear exactly what the quarrel is about. Also, whether we're in our reserved mode or our expressive mode, we can be especially effective by voicing the other person's insights, motivations, and feelings, not just our own.

Think of it: The conflict may not be resulting from ill will or mistakes. Often it's simply that we're all different. No two people see the world quite the same. There's an axiom that says, "Be yourself. Everyone else has already been taken." We can stretch that to letting others be themselves too. In fact, our perceptions are seldom completely accurate. Yes, it may be hard to wake up to different truths, views, feelings, needs, and preferences, but it can also be enlightening, even refreshing. "Hey, you and I are unique. You like to keep moving. I like to take breaks." In a conflict, our brain often has us so focused on winning that we don't explore. We don't realize that there might be an angle new to us, one that might give us pause. We might actually see this angle as legitimate, even if we don't fully agree.

Listening is good—and so is a caring expression. Some of us

hold back viewpoints and feelings like hoarders. That can be good, but not always. It may be important to express the differing views, to put them all out there. There may be convictions we need to express in words, maybe even with action. In certain situations and with certain people you may lean toward being silent. You may be more reserved, even a lurker. There may be certain people you steer clear of. Then as a result of your silence, the other person may also lose the chance to express perspectives and feelings that may be opposite and important.

In some situations, we may default to our "reserved" skills—pulling back and listening. We're receptive, asking for clarifications. That's good, but we might at our quiet times miss out on rich ideas on both sides—including our own. True, many folks are not ready to compare differences; in fact, most of us have a compulsion to eliminate differences. So yes, of course, at times it is wise to stay silent. Nonetheless, sometimes silence is not the lesser of two evils, it's wrong. Some of us may need to practice being more expressive, and not settle for being only a good, happy listener.

The opposite can be true for times where our default is to be the articulate and expressive authority. We may forget all about being curious, listening, and drawing out the other person. A usually very-expressive friend commented that someone stuck in their expressive mode enjoys it. And he knows from his experience that someone stuck in a reticent mode loves the familiar listening mode, for a while. He calls these interacting phenomena "mutual default" comfort zones. Going in circles this way is common, but as you may have experienced, it can get us more stuck, not less. The more-expressive one goes on expressing and the more-reticent one goes on listening. With two expressive people, the less expressive one goes into listening. So the expressive one doesn't get important new knowledge and the reticent one's ideas pile up inside, sometimes to the point of exploding.

Getting past mutual default cycles may take a mutual learning process. But someone has to get unstuck enough to start that. We can train ourselves—and if possible, our partners—to work toward enjoying expressiveness and reserve at the same time.

When we're in our default cycle together, the idea of equal time, even just a bit of more-equal time, might seem novel and awkward. Broaching this subject starts a whole new discussion and exposure to uncomfortable adjustments and new discomfort zones.

This is a pattern worth breaking, but hard to break. People enjoy their set patterns and breaking them seems impossible. Another person, who describes herself as an expressive, said "Take it from me, this listening and not talking, so I can be mindful of equal time, it's a bear. I wonder if it actually can be easier if both are working on it—assuming they agree to try and allow some checking of each other."

How can colleagues and couples ease into this strange new equal-time territory? I sometimes suggest that the person in the reticent, questioning mode say "I have some questions, but to make our conversation more equal: Are there any questions you'd like to ask me?" That gives the habitual talker an invitation to ask and listen. It turns the vicious cycle into a virtuous cycle.

Roberto Assagioli, founder of Psychosynthesis, long ago scribbled on a notepad the key element in stopping that sort of vicious cycle: simply reversing one of its parts. I discovered his note saved in his Florence, Italy, study, which is still arranged just as he had it and available for research such as I was doing. Vicious cycles in relationships can be pernicious. They often feel like stumbling blocks, immoveable. But we only have to choose one piece. Say the more expressive partner stops identifying with only his or her expressive side. That means they stop triggering silence and nods to invite the other into the dialogue. Or the reserved partner stops identifying with only his or her reserved side, and speaks up. Again, that interrupts the other's endless talk, especially if they discuss the pattern and both keep watch. Simply reversing one pole has saved me and lots of clients from vicious cycles.

We all have both expressive and reserved skills. However, in moments of conflict at home or work our reptile brains tend to use one or the other. Either it's fight (trying to knock down our friend's or loved one's wrong idea), or flight (backing off and yielding the whole spotlight, ignoring our precious values).

No benefits emerge unless we learn to take our focus off the affront coming from outside us and learn to forget about arguing. We need a moment of mindfulness, a look at our inner experience of our own brain's knee-jerk reaction. That mindfulness is space to embrace our preference, which the reaction was defending, and space for the Anger-Makeover process to bathe us in a deep value. No, we don't always have to voice this positive value, but the process helps us dig down, find the value, and celebrate it. It may seem surprising that we can use our sharp, shallow reactions to seek out our values, but that's what this book demonstrates.

Wouldn't it be great if there were something simple and quick to do whenever we feel angry, when we think the best we can do is wish everything would cool down? What if when we're in the grip of a reaction there was a way to get clear about how to respond? There is. Stop. Pause. Sense your body's distress, and settle it using the five clear steps of the Anger-Makeover process.

These steps spell a word, **POWER**. Personal power is your goal. It's the change you want. By starting with **P,** you picture the problem to separate the event that just happened from how your body and psyche reacted to it. The rest of the letters take you inside yourself to transform your anger and panic into power. When you **O**wn your physical and emotional feelings, you switch from the external event to learning about your internal reactions and process. Exploring **W,** you want what you want, carrying the transformation forward. You may immediately notice a change in your body, such as less tension and more solidness. With **E,** you enjoy and embrace your values, pulling up the inner knowing underneath your want. You may feel your body come into its own as you feel your personal power. You are now ready to **R**eview your range of options. You already have more than when you started.

New Possibilities

You may feel a change immediately and find it easier to balance your listening with your talking, your reserve with your self-expression. Added to that, even if you never do agree with your friend, you feel positive values of your own that you may never have fully experienced and enjoyed. And it may be easier to embrace values on both sides. We get more ideas when we don't neglect one side. And just imagine if both values could combine forces!

A reader used the Anger Makeover, and even though she and her friend still didn't agree, she felt the benefits. She said her friend was clearly very bright, was a staunch libertarian, a trained lawyer and engineer—and "nonetheless a big pain." She added that

> He loves to invite debate and rant. I have come to realize his single biggest value is freedom to do whatever. We have been known to (um, after a couple of drinks) . . . start to shout at each other. After our spouses have kicked us under the table, we have to find something silly and fun we both agree on.

After using the Anger Makeover, she saw Harvey differently.

> We are better about this now. I really have caught myself and realized where he is coming from. I still don't agree but I can respect his viewpoints a little more.

But to have even that limited success regularly we have to be willing to develop new abilities, because the natural tendency is to get locked in on the brain's hothead mode. That can be extremely hard to get out of—at least all the way out. To move past the anger-reaction culture we're swimming in, the quicksand in which our world seems stuck, requires a strong, skillful decision. We need to develop the ability to stop being in that reactive mode. Yes, the fact that the knee-jerk reaction is connected to the pleasure-seeking part of our brain makes it hard, but in the end, by working to get past those too-pleasant reactions, you will actually feel much better. As we use the Anger-Makeover steps, we find a much richer reward system than the one linked to our standard-issue reptilian brain. And by using the steps regularly, we develop important mental muscles.

That may sound daunting, but anyone can practice and learn what I am sharing, even if I'm still practicing and learning it myself. When confronted, we often notice what's happening and feel, "Whoa! This is a very strong experience." That's the time to back away, enough to start hunting: "What exactly is this, and where is it registering in my body?" That's the mindfulness that gives you a bit of space, and hope of getting get past resentment or argument.

It's at that moment that the Anger Makeover almost effortlessly moves you toward your affirming, inclusive, non-judging Self. And that opens up endless options.

You can enjoy a value. Acknowledge a truth new to you. Compare complementary values glowing in opposite ideas. Discuss rather than push or run. Speak articulately and purposefully and listen with curiosity and excitement. You can even create a new possibility such as some practical, creative joint enterprise. Each of these opens to yet more options.

This book addresses three levels of conflict:

Reptilian conflict. In this very basic knee-jerk conflict, we identify with our hothead reaction. This is an anger-fear process. Sometimes it works, but humans overuse it. In fact, many or most of us are addicted to it. Even the reptiles aren't as addicted to it as we are. They use it when it serves their survival.

Mindful non-conflict. This level can help us get to the next level. Here we go inside and do some work with our impulse rather than engage with the other person or before we engage. We identify with our best self, and from there we look at our anger reaction as if from a distance. We've refrained from arguing or debating with the friend or colleague, or we've stopped the conflict. This does take conflict way past the basic knee-jerk level. It dodges the fruitless win-lose habit, because stepping back from the anger allows us to go inside and apply the Anger Makeover. First of all, we want to find inner power. This stage works, as far as it goes. We get away from the conflict and identify with spirit, love, and respect while converting the anger preferences and values, which are self-empowering. That's a magical change inside us, and the relationship with our colleague or loved one is less likely to deteriorate.

Yet the relationship may not coalesce as it might if we go to the next level, re-engaging and defining our differences and resolving the conflict in a mutually beneficial process of growing together. That next level of resolution may still be an open possibility, if we can go there, so this second-level pull-back is a very good start.

The first edition of this book came this far, but I have since gotten a better idea of how spirit can interact in human life. Our relationship to spirit grows gradually, whether in stages or leaps. So how and whether the next, third level of conflict works for us may depend on our beliefs or level of growth. It may come in stages or levels of its own.

Mindful Spirit conflict. Here, once we have looked at our anger reaction from a bit of a distance and have gone from powerless annoyance to a sense of power, it helps if we can expand to realize we are part of a nonjudgmental awareness that we know is already present and always present. As that inclusive Self, we hold close as an ally the anger inside that we have begun to transform. We identify with what you might call our spirit Self while at the same time we go forward, joined with the reactive, concerned side of us. We're like an adult embracing an alert, stirred up, focused youth. It's as if we are guiding the youth through the respectful-conflict process. Spirit and the angry or concerned part stick together as a team, and look at the conflict situation. Together we sort out the ways we and the coworker or loved one are not bad but simply different and have different preferences and values. In level two, mindful non-conflict, we have already used the Anger Makeover and looked inside, into our reactive part, and found enlightening preferences and power-values. That has eased us into the much-needed awareness of our spirit Self. We are working within ourself, with the energy of our anger's preferences and values, and also with the other person.

Inside us, this is conflict with reverence both for our Spirit Self and for our angry, alert, already enlightening part. Outwardly, this is conflict with reverence for the person important to us and for the differences. We want to define, not judge, the differences. Because we have used the Anger-Makeover practice to work with the reactive part inside us, bringing out the enlightening preferences and powerful values that were buried in it, we are able to listen and work for loving, respectful differentiation. We have a chance of listening to each other and teaching each other.

It took me a long time to learn about Mindful Spirit conflict, so to be as clear as possible let me make a few further attempts to describe this third level of conflict. At this third level we continue to be the Self or Spirit we are, while we lovingly embrace a reactive part of us, and we can then engage outwardly in effective, noncontrolling conflict. We move into being our nonjudgmental spirit self but without avoiding the feelings we feel and the differences we see as we engage. By moving the anger feelings into personal power, we can approach our friend with gentle, respectful strength. We caringly join with the person we're close to and angry at, not to change each other, but to define together how we are different and what we may have to offer each other.

Or put it this way: We identify with our best Self and at the same time respectfully corral our stirred-up side and work with it, so that as a unified and worthy team we can focus on the issue, to differentiate. Our spirit side keeps us nonjudgmental, and our anger side keeps us focused. As a team we listen and open ourselves to having our friend speak up. We listen to our voice and get ourselves to speak up, too.

When we take the time and effort to be our nonjudgmental Spirit, we include and transform our reactive self. In conjunction with that energetic, reactive self, we work through the conflict. That means we respectfully, lovingly make ample space for our colleague or loved one's differences and for our own differences. As the spirit that we are, we embrace our reaction, those heightened feelings and differences, and then reverently exchange viewpoints with someone close to us—with interest, care, and self-care.

Let me try saying it one more way. We find inner power in allying nonjudgmental Self with our anger's preferences and values. We don't just flee from anger feelings and take refuge in Spirit, love, and respect. We experience the power in our Spirit as well as the positive power locked behind our emotional response. This combination makes it possible for us to engage with our family member or colleague humbly and honestly.

We've all succumbed to letting anger make things worse. We can use it to evolve. The world is regressing to uncontrolled anger and to all sorts of reptilian, brawling conflict. Things get stuck at the lowest level—simple fear-based fight or flight or freeze or fawn. This makes us indulge in lots of psychological and physical violence.

This book is about moving away from knee-jerk conflict and rising to at least mindful non-conflict. Instead of being engulfed in your knee-jerk reaction, you simply stop to look at it. Looking as your loving, observer self, you find the positive strength that's buried in the anger. If you can't yet bring yourself to engage with your partner or colleague, or can't use tools, you at least stop using weapons. After all, if you remember when anyone, including a workmate or sibling or life partner, has used psychological weapons such as blame, accusation, and the cold shoulder on you, think how unproductive or counterproductive that was. And further, physical weapons such as hitting or shoving or worse are way beyond useless.

This book points us toward an ideal beyond non-conflict. Here, as you learn to be your best self, you listen to your own inner irritation with love and find the positive energy in it. You may even be able to join with a friend or colleague who very recently felt like an opponent. Together you may be able to look for the positives on both sides. There are always positive values hidden in the irritations on both sides. Once you find the positives, you may be able to combine these positive opposite qualities creatively. You may form something new that is satisfying to both parties. That would mean you'd have taken the anger itself and turned it into sharing and health. You'd have pushed the relationship forward instead of backward.

Watch for Brushfires of Anger

For 13 years I co-led divorce, separation, and personal growth seminars to help people grow after painful separations. Many participants were heartbroken that their partner had given up on the relationship. I understood. I was no stranger to relationship mistakes myself. I had prematurely given up on friends and relatives.

What is a key reason for so many people giving up a close relationship?

There's a thing called a non-empathy state. Neither empathy nor interest in differences even occurs to us. We've already charged forward, but it's just to be right, not to save our life. We are sure the other person is being nasty. We don't always see when we're the one being nasty, when we're blaming, or being right. The results of this? A big reason humans have a 50-percent divorce rate, fading friendships, and a divided world is that we are so blind to the devastation of knee-jerk reactions .

By watching out for brushfires, couples could avoid separations and have more fun. When annoyed, they could stop, reflect, and—if they're quick enough to catch themselves—not blurt out the correction their knee-jerk brain ordered. Or, when they're not quick enough and it seems they missed another chance at avoiding being obnoxious, it's still not too late to back up and revise the response. Reflecting on run-of-the-mill differences and then responding instead of reacting offers big benefits. It makes relationships blossom.

Here are three typical, more-or-less subtly complaining comments that a reader offered. I'll follow up with two good tricks that beat complaining. By simply putting in a phrase like "I'd prefer" or "I think things go better when," you can soften the criticism and make known your stable preferences and values.

1. A friend asked about a comment like, "Why call the place a disaster? Can't you relax if there are newspapers on the counter?" That could become "When it's something like newspapers on the counter, I

believe things will go better if we relax and work out a solution."

2. The comment "When will you learn to put your dishes in the sink?" could become "I'd prefer if we both put our dishes in the sink."

3. A comment like "You know this event is important to me; so why aren't you ready to go on time?" could become simply, "When an event is important to me, I want you to make sure to be ready on time."

To get a feel for the subtle difference, you can see how you feel, first imagining you're the speaker, then imagining you're the friend or colleague listening. You may notice where in your body you feel the criticism, and where in your body you feel the expression of preference or value. When your body feels relief or excitement or strength, you may be sensing the gentle power we have over brushfires. Using the Anger Makeover trains you to lay down a safer, more-solid foundation for the relationship. You find it easier to come up with your personal preferences and values.

That discovery can transform hard moments between couples or coworkers and pull people closer, which in turn may gradually give them a foothold for improving their whole gamut of social relationships. I would agree that even one-on-one relationships are not simple, though they may be the simplest kind. Assagioli (1976, pp. 66-69) reminded us people have multiple subpersonalities. Sometimes subpersonalities make an interaction confusing, almost amusing to an observer, as if we're struggling to work out things with more than one person.

Still, our intimate relationships are the place to start our very important quest: to accept conflicts and make them gentle and effective. Couple relationships are usually our most powerful and lasting ones, and the ones in which we spend most time, so they keep giving us fresh chances to practice and do better.

Of course, it's great when both partners or colleagues watch carefully to see what's working and what's not. But even one person can watch and get things working better. Even if your partner is not quite so willing, you can still lead the way. You can make it a point to pause your brain's action, use the Anger-Makeover process, and start changing a knee-jerk habit into a habit of bringing helpful responses to the surface. Yes, it's true frustrations are contagious, but so are positive impulses, fun feelings, and exciting visions.

Moments of day-to-day irritation are the times when the Anger Makeover gives you great mileage. In fact, as soon as you learn to gather the positive energy waiting inside workaday knee-jerk impulses, you are on a whole new road. For the rest of your life, whether your anger feels small or big, it works for you instead of against you.

Fanning our small anger fires works against us. Instead, we could transform them—use them to shine a light inward on our preferences. When rants by people trigger more anger, including ours, we often make matters worse. We could be taking note that our brain is reacting and shutting down our empathy. If we keep fires going, we add to the debilitating stress that is everywhere.

Even when the spark is a small annoyance hitting us, such annoyances can shut down the precious caring parts of our brain. They do this just in case it's a real threat hitting us. Caring about the other person would slow down our fight-or-flight response. Unfortunately, when the friendly and gentle parts of our brains get shut down, it then feels like it's time for weapons such as sarcasm. So our tools vanish from sight, such as patience and talking things through. It's sad when we're with a coworker or loved one and our larger, loving purpose gets blurred or vanishes. We can't think of our rich, effective words, looks, or gestures. We're locked in to a reflex emotion. Whether hot or ice-cold, that emotion makes it hard to stop. We don't feel like waiting long enough to identify our positive values. The wild yet natural instinct buries the values. Ironically, the instinct is fighting for the values, but prevents us from identifying and voicing them. No wonder it's so hard to pause long enough to identify the positive values: The emotions are demanding. When we learn ways to pause, we give ourselves a chance to use the Anger Makeover to recalibrate, so we can interact amicably and with heart.

But it's a volatile mix, that scary spark from outside touching the tinder within us. There it goes, our primitive brain, always on alert for something scary. Someone recently commented to me, "People love to build on negativity." I love negativity too. When something gets us worked up, the excitement of fanning fires feels so pleasurable, so satisfying. That's humans' negativity bias. We are much more aware of negative events than positive. The brain goes, "Got it! I'll watch out for that." Or, "Him I hate, and it feels so good." Negativity is tied to pleasure, and it enhances the value of the Anger Makeover. We get to play with the negativity we love so much, and we get to turn it into personal power. Coming to love personal power even more than the negativity you were feeling at first: that is what the Anger Makeover is specifically about. There's instant enjoyment in building some-thing positive from the initial negative mistake.

People waste more time in the negative side of their brain than they realize. It's chronic. One reason is the hot-cold empathy gap (Van Boven, L., Lowenstein, G., Dunning, D., Nordgren, L. 2013). We don't grasp how hot the negative state is. Impulse takes over and drives us so convincingly that during the negative state we forget sanity, goals, and rational decisions. Then, after we get back in the everyday cold state, we feel perfectly goal-oriented and sane. We can't remember how dominant the hot state was. So even though the primitive brain is always on hyper alert for danger, we forget to stay ready to pause and take an easy breath before considering our response.

Why do hot states show up so routinely? And why is it important for us to look to the long term in changing these old tension habits? Our ancient brain is protecting our needs, as it always has. The needs we feel are deep and they go way back: the need for inclusion vs. banishment from the clan; the need for a home territory vs. being invaded by immigrants; the need for food vs. slow starvation; and the need for love and fulfillment. We feel every need on every level of Maslow's hierarchy of needs. Just the shadow of a loss of any of these turns panic on instantly —and turns off calm, reason, and compassion. That can damage a bond permanently. It's complicated by different kinds of frustration intolerance: A friend said, "From an early age, I guess I expected the world to be arranged as I desired. No wonder I keep getting frustrated."

A Grudge of Mine

Paradoxically all this happens even with loved ones in our clan. I still get nudged by a grudge against one of my relatives and his whole clan—which is by nature part of my clan. I sensed that this relative and offspring of his were contemptuous and distant. Was that true, or just leftovers from inner judgmental reactions of mine? I have to admit, I'm not sure my siblings share my judgments.

I can improve that relationship magically, even though that uncle is long dead. How? I can get in the habit of noticing every urge to fan into a brushfire any spark of judgment I may feel toward him. I can create a habit of consistently pausing, flashing a gentle, grateful smile toward the dutiful, protective, instinctual urge, and questioning its accuracy. The Anger Makeover can get me free from that old, constantly remanufactured bag of stress.

I hope we can eventually prevent emotional forest fires in our larger world, with its overwhelming potentials for support and absurd capacities for war. This constant manufacturing of stress, often out of mere sparks, is needless. In fact many, maybe most so-called sparks were not even sparks in the first place, just glitter. I'm staying on the watch for false alarms from my ever-alert knee-jerk instincts, because humans turn even glitter into fires. Fortunately, when we start noticing every time we make something worse, we get a better sense of how it keeps happening. This teaches us how to avoid being stuck with an imagined situation that we mistakenly turned into an issue. Better to replace searing heat with nurturing warmth.

Don't Fan the Spark. Absorb Its Light

By not creating flames out of sparks or glitter, we stop inviting the kind of stress that causes inflammation and dementia. It would be apt to continue—to repeat itself in family, community, nation, and world. Have you noticed more nastiness every day, everywhere? It has been building for eons. Now, what if I paid attention every time I got the urge to fan a spark, or to pretend the spark didn't come from inside me? In the moment, the spark or issue seems like such a big deal. It feels so urgent. Yes, many times someone's comment or silence may seem like an invitation to an argument, but that doesn't make it a real invitation. By far, most sparks could be gently put out or consciously left alone to die out.

It's still pretty much a secret that some threatening sparks may even turn out to carry much-needed light. That's a main insight of this book. After you make pausing a habit, you might be able to feel appreciation for good features you start to see in the sparks. There's something in them that I love. It's energy I could use and thank myself or my loved one for. Once we learn to look for the light in each of those sparks, using the Anger Makeover, we may feel a little more hope and get a good look at the benefits of being alert. Instead of letting our stress ratchet up regularly, we can start lowering it regularly. We could develop deeper bonding with a friend or loved one.

Discussions Can Work When You Agree on Their Purpose

Many times when it is important to discuss annoying differences, everyone gets mad. However, especially in a close relationship, it helps first to agree on the purpose of the discussion. If either party's goal is simply to get the other to think or feel as they do, it's not a discussion but an argument. What fans the flame? Pushing for sameness without realizing it. We think we are working for agreement, but that usually means for our colleague or loved one to agree with us. It may feel like coming to agreement is a reasonable goal, but that's an illusion if it means we want someone to simply be like us, to see the matter the way we do.

There is an evolutionary purpose for exchanges, and I sincerely hope we are ready as a species to achieve this. The purpose is not to bludgeon the other person into agreeing with us. It's not to erase differences, but to appreciate differences, make them clearer. Erasing them only puts them on lockdown. Wouldn't you be more likely to sign on to such an exchange if the purpose were to help brilliant differences survive, even interact? For combatants to pledge to stay a loving team? To celebrate the passion of both persons and combine the unique wisdom of both?

You Can't Homogenize, So Differentiate

Drs. Ellyn Bader and Peter Pearson (couplesinstitute.com) call such an exchange differentiation. It's miraculous. Having an attitude of respect introduces light. Simply seeing how you and your partner are different, instead of right or wrong, makes your opposite positions more acceptable. You can appreciate what's valuable on each side. Working as a couple is similar to working with subpersonalities inside yourself: You can make space for both parties. This is a huge relief, especially for the person who hasn't been getting heard. This relief throws open the gate dramatically to new deals, even synthesis. It's heartening for anyone to have her or his gifts and values recognized. Suddenly you can agree on new ways of interacting. This can save marriages. There's less confusion, and interactions have a new focus.

Both Expressive and Reserved:
Being Smart About Aggression and Passiveness

So how am I dealing with anger? Well, is it showing up as out-of-control aggression, whether physical or psychological? Or perhaps as out-of-control passiveness? If so, get professional help. Is it too much expressiveness and not enough reserve? Or is it too much reserve and not enough expressiveness? Our lives and varying situations need to become consistently a synthesis of expressiveness and reserve, not a lurch into one or the other. The Psychosynthesis and Education Trust of London published an article by Assagioli called "What Is Synthesis?" In it Assagioli painted the large picture from psychic life. "As in organic life, in psychic life we find a rhythmic alternating of two opposing principles, that of extraversion and of introversion. . . . A harmonious succession of these movements should constitute the rhythm of life. And to reach this rhythm an art of living is necessary" (http://www.kennethsorensen.dk/en/what-is-synthesis). Assagioli's Psychosynthesis was a whole movement, an effective art of living.

In dealing with anger, we are all equipped with skills in both expression and reserve, but at moments of possible crisis, knee-jerk shortcuts naturally kick in—versions of fight or flight. Our lower brain, in a split-second, must twist our expressiveness into aggression, or our reserve into passivity. That kind of impulse to panic is normal and routine, and with repetition we can routinely switch back to employing effective expressive and reserved skills. We don't have to yield to fight or flight.

But above all, if your anger gets out of control, get help fast. If it's too hard to give up aggressive and passive impulses like teaching a lesson, or revenge, or control, this book by itself is not enough, although it may help. Maybe we all could use a therapist's or coach's help along with this book. After all, these impulses go back to pre-human history. The word anger stems from the Latin *angere,* and the Greek *anchein,* both of which mean "to strangle." This makes me wonder if the ancients suspected what's now clear. The emotion of anger can constrict and strangle the angry person's own blood vessels, resulting eventually in angina and strokes. Surely they knew people may feel the urge to strangle someone, even their partners. Anger has confused and misled people enough to mix its meaning with revenge. That mix-up may come from ancient times, but to this day, there are people all over the world who, when they hear "accept your anger," think it means just speak and act on raw anger feelings. You know there will always be those who gleefully buy into revenge, forcing, or excluding an opponent they consider empty-headed or pure evil.

Can we undo that confusion? It's vast. Can we instead choose consistently not to stay on automatic with anger? The anger impulse, normal as it is, is of course not just not an excuse for physical violence. It's also not an excuse for the psychological violence of disrespect, nastiness, stonewalling, shut-downs, or judgment. Really? None of these? None.

Then what is the impulse to anger for? Is it fundamentally a healthy impulse? Saying yes signals hope, because it encourages us not to try to get rid of the anger, but to routinely transform the animal impulse into a human response. That's doable, in a variety of ways. Assagioli wrote about doing therapy with a man subject to fits of rage, and he devised physical methods to transform the physical energy of the rage. Transforming the animal impulse into a human response is the essence of the Anger-Makeover method and this book.

Can we hope to change our world? "We are capable of the most horrendous crimes and most sublime acts," said Piero Ferrucci. "Neither of these two potentials is established enough to allow us to define it as a dominant trait of human nature." He added, "It is up to us."

How about if we start with a tiny part of ourselves? We can train ourselves so each sudden anger moment is a wakeup call. From that vantage point we can observe how we're experiencing this anger moment. Our brain is pliable. We don't have to let the automatically triggered reaction, that impulse, decide our ongoing behavior. Being mindful of such impulses and questioning each impulse's stubborn message gives us a chance to make our own choice. We switch to discovery, not to inaction. We discover respectful, interactive responses.

And we don't have to settle for just not being inappropriate with anger. With the help of this book, each of us can actively use anger feelings to help us find and put to use unique positive powers waiting in our dark insides. Yes, every angry feeling is an opportunity to step back and get unscrambled from our ancient history and build up precious relationships, not rip them up. When things get really heated, it's hard to remember to use the anger feelings to find underlying soul qualities. I look back and see the times I've gotten exploited by the anger feelings and given up on someone because I didn't put the feelings to *use*. Maybe all of us have. Patiently learning to make a better choice is worth the practice it takes.

One big reason this is possible is that the Anger Makeover gives immediate rewards. The positive feedback helps us look straight at knee-jerk anger impulses, not ignore them. It helps us disidentify from them, feel immediate relief from the pressure, and make use of their energy. I was talking to Ingrid, a woman familiar with the Anger-Makeover process. I mentioned that longtime confusion between "anger" and "strangle," the linking of anger and violence. "If anger means to strangle," she said, "that would leave two options, to strangle ourselves or others. We don't have to do either."

Ingrid knew the Anger Makeover is a way to find better alternatives and show respect as well as be direct. This book is for folks who don't want to strangle their feelings, blood vessels, their kids, or the boss. I asked Ingrid why she keeps using the Anger Makeover.

"It clarifies my thinking," she said. "It puts things in perspective. It helps me resolve problems otherwise not resolvable." As examples, she mentioned hopelessness about a global issue, or lingering anger with someone she'll never see again. It helps her feel good about herself, about the things she believes are important in life. "I go from anger to power and get clear with people," she says. "It opens me to positive change."

This book was originally focused on the times we want to swallow or discount anger. That's just half of it, but when we are overly reserved or passive, the following strategies may be helpful:

- *Make room for anger as natural,* but be skeptical about its too-firm impulses. Don't scold yourself, or worry, or pretend the reactions don't exist. Just always check whether you believe what those impulses say, and make your own choice about whether and how to act on them.
- *Constructively explore impulses.* Five simple Anger-Makeover steps deliver the means for this and cut confusion.
- *Unearth the positive values under your anger.* Each of these values is a distinct taste of who you are.
- *Consider ways to speak up.* Silence may be appropriate, but when you can gently define your unique self, you're unwrapping a gift for yourself as well as your partner.

Make the World Safe for Conflict

One friend said the Anger Makeover can "make the world safe for conflict." Read on, if at times you shy away from your anger and are looking for some way to resolve inner conflicts about anger, or if you sometimes get a little trigger-happy with anger. If you finally understand that creative conflicts are a part of life; if you want to turn your fear about anger into feeling confident and competent, even feeling constructively passionate; if you're ready to start resolving more of those natural, daily conflicts that keep coming up at home and at work; if you want to connect better with your loved ones, acquaintances, strangers, and the organizations you're part of about differences that threaten to disconnect you, read on. You'll get a feeling for how effective the tools in this book are.

Control Someone?
Or Use the Anger Makeover to Find Your Best Self?

Oh, wouldn't we all love to take over someone's executive function and make changes for them? We just can't. They have their own path. But we can use our anger to guide us toward loving the unique insights we get from our vantage point. That makes it easier to let people make clearer decisions for themselves. Anger in ordinary life is not meant for controlling other people, even when we feel absolutely sure we're right. You've heard people tell you how angry they are, as if how angry they are proved how right they are. All it proves is that their brain's built-in sensors and self-protections are triggering well. They could use the anger to find out what information they have that might be helpful, such as where they stand and what they want to accomplish.

Since each person's perceptions and wants are unique, both you and your associate have valuable knowledge for each other. You've seen how panic, pressure, and yelling can backfire and hurt a cause instead of helping. Sometimes when we think our anger is controlling people, it's just that they for once know what we think, and respect it. It feels good to see people being gentle instead of forcing, and exercising clean power by sharing their unique perspective. It's good not to let the anger talk, and instead step back, especially if we remember to speak up about our preferences. Besides, even when the anger is hogging the spotlight, there is a rich array of other feelings too, colorful information to mention besides the anger. We have love, worry, hope, sadness, and respect.

Moral Convictions: Do We Avoid Them?
Or Prepare to Use Them With Great Care?

So, does moving away from misplaced fight-or-flight habits mean we lie down and play dead, and give up causes important to us? No. So then, is it that we need to switch from pissed to passionate? Yes, in that we need to keep turning our impulse function from reactive autopilot to proactive desire. Pissed by itself doesn't work. Passionate gives us new wings, as long as it doesn't make us inflexible.

Psychologist Linda Skitka and her colleagues at the University of Chicago did research which she discussed on NPR's *Hidden Brain: Moral Combat*. This alerted me to the way moral convictions may expand our energy yet may also close our minds. The human race has its work cut out for it just calibrating the possible impacts of moral imperatives—which ones are real, and how to respond or not respond to them. Some people end up distancing themselves socially and physically from friends or groups that have dissimilar convictions. Tolerance, trust, and good will may become difficult, which makes a compromise or synthesis harder when it might help. That insight is complex and daunting. For me, it opens up a stirring albeit thorny question: Are compromises (exchanging benefits) and synthesis (joining forces) always helpful?

The answer depends on what the stakes are. Anger with moral conviction is tricky. Skitka points out that a moral conviction is a subjective psychological state. That tells me a given moral conviction isn't necessarily a universal principle, although some are. As you may have noticed in your relationships, the validity of convictions varies widely. That's worth remembering, because in some cases we may be the one holding on too tightly to a conviction. We are certain it is objective reality and certain that a friend's conviction is not. Blocking out any opponent friend's moral convictions may be risky. We risk missing out on valid information, losing respect, and ending a good connection. Our reptilian brain, already and always in fight-or-flight mode, may be blocking empathy and thought.

Causes and passion seem to fit together well, yet as you have seen, your passion often does not change the mind of a friend or family member who has an opposing opinion. What is in your power is to change your rigidity, when appropriate. And that changes you. That is closely related to our working to change from anger to shared personal power, which I'm encouraging in this book.

But wait. Didn't we say some moral convictions in fact are universal and therefore moral imperatives? Certainly. And that is what makes this so tricky. At times we *are* our brothers' and sisters' keepers. If, as we've seen, moral passions put us in thorny territory, we very much need a process like the Anger Makeover to help us find our way through safely.

You can see why picayune issues in relationships are the first place I want us to put into practice the Anger Makeover. They are easier and come up often with loved ones, friends, and colleagues. When I'm teaching workshops, I encourage people to tackle small issues first, not big ones. This is hard for them to do when a big issue is weighing on their mind, but they thank me later, because they discover how easy it is to get stuck and discouraged. Releasing our knee-jerk irritations comes first. Once we learn the Anger-Makeover steps, they boost our effectiveness so down the line we can learn to approach the challenges of restoring respectful politics and rebuilding fractured humanity.

But does this process really help with big issues as well as the picayune ones? Yes. We benefit from feeling and inspecting not just our anger but our preferences and values, including strong values. Still, let's practice on easy problems for now. Then we can use this process to hurl weight and strength into our actions for causes that are not picayune but vitally important to us. This book will help us bring not just anger to our work for a cause, but also passion, skill—and when needed, might. Some causes are real and truly big.

We are going to need to combine goodness with great skill when using our power. After escaping Buchenwald and Auschwitz, Elie Wiesel in 1986 decried the lack of passion and action that the world had displayed in his youth when the Nazi butchery was grinding forward. "How naïve we were," he said. "The world did know and remained silent."

Yes, I continue to recommend movement toward synthesis when possible, meaning searching out opposing positive forces and putting them together. But that is not intended to endorse any limp sort of neutrality, slowness, or silence that ignores serious injustice and harmful aggression.

"Neutrality helps the oppressor, never the victim," said Wiesel. "Silence encourages the tormentor, never the tormented."

The Anger Makeover moves us from our anger into being roused by our personal power. Only then can we decide on the most fitting speech or action. Also, in my colleagues' and my observation, the Anger Makeover boosts relationships. The way to steadily change bad habits is by practicing good ones. We can easily practice good habits today at home and work, and see immediate benefits. And tomorrow, when the time comes for taking crucially important action, those same habits of pausing and skillfully thinking things through will make all the difference. Meanwhile, this transforming of how we manage day-to-day conflicts cuts down on half-baked conflicts that mar and even devastate relationships. And the big perils of our times may soon summon the effective habits we are building here.

Who Can or Can't Use the Anger Makeover?
Three Everyday Examples

First let me illustrate who might benefit more and who less from this Anger Makeover. Later I'll explain in depth how the process works. Right now, here's a quick look at June, George, and Cliff.

Unselfish June: Can the Anger Makeover Benefit Her?

There's a saying in the corporate world, "You get angry, you get fired." Here's a workplace example of how using the Anger Makeover can save the day. June had started a new job at a large computer servicing company. In her early twenties, she had just learned the process. It was helping her through situations that in the past might have disrupted her feelings of well-being, even her employment.

She said, "I got really embarrassed and ticked off with Marcie, my supervisor. I was getting on-the-job training, learning to help customers solve rather complicated problems.

"Anyway, I bobbled a question and a customer complained. Marcie decided I needed what is called supportive training. She sent word that I was to meet with Karl, the staff trainer. It felt like punishment. I felt humiliated."

"All it meant was that I got to spend an hour chatting with Karl about my weak areas, discuss technicalities of fielding questions, and brainstorm ways he might help me improve my work with customers. Still, I felt like calling Marcie and saying, 'Hey, you high-handed so-and-so. You don't have to *shake* me into shape. I'm not some lazy kid. I've been studying and working hard.'"

Some people would say, "Well, why not tell Marcie that? It sounds like a good idea. You're supposed to get it off your chest." Marcie would have felt hurt and threatened, and with good reason. But June, as I observed, defaults to her reserved skills in conflicts more than her expressive skills, so she wasn't about to say the wrong thing. In fact, in the past she wouldn't have said anything. At times like this she typically would have brooded and stewed—and so she'd have felt hurt and resentful every time she saw Marcie striding around the office.

Instead, June had a tool, the Anger Makeover, to use anytime. It was ready in her head.

"Instead of just shutting down," June went on, "or saying something resentful, I took myself through the Anger-Makeover process. I used lulls between customers to think and write. In minutes, I felt more like an adult woman again instead of a hurt little girl. I understood what was important to me and saw Marcie clearly. She had done her best. She was really on my side.

"Most of all, by first going through the Anger-Makeover process, I had cleared up for myself what I was most angry about. It was not that Marcie had sent me to supportive training. That wasn't a bad idea. What got my goat was that she hadn't consulted with me first. This new insight surprised me. My anger was about something different from what I originally had thought: not what she had done, but how she had done it.

"That took me to a whole other area, Marcie's supervisory style. Yes, something is wrong there. Still, she is clearly the best and most conscientious of all the supervisors—and probably of all the personnel in that company, from CEO on down. Maybe someday, I thought, I will talk to her about her style, but now would be bad timing. At least I had thought it through and felt better. I still wasn't ready to talk, but at least I didn't yell or brood. And I saw that I have something to say in a case like that, maybe something like, 'Marcie, I think your idea is a good one, for me to take some time with Karl in the training room. I just want you to know, I'd have felt more respected if you had discussed it with me in person first. I'd have agreed.'

"I'm still learning, so I guess getting it clear in my own head was progress. I felt better. Next time I'll say something, but this time I decided that at some point I might talk to Marcie. For the time being I'd wait. I did pretty good, though.

"Patrick is a coworker who had been nearby when the original mistake happened. I talked with him to get his slant on it. He reassured me that I was doing a good job. He understood why I had become confused and given the wrong advice. 'That,' he said with a grin, 'is an easy mistake for someone to make at your stage of training.' So I got to talk about it a bit and felt relief.

"Also, I had clarified my own values. First, that it's important for a supervisor to consult with certain subordinates rather than just give them orders. Second, that it's important that a training program (including on-the-job training) be precise, not sloppy, and include extra help and drill on the more confusing areas. After I had finished with my Anger-Makeover writing about my feelings, I still felt a bit shaken, but I also felt basically secure and more self-respecting and respectful of Marcie."

Yes, the Anger Makeover Can Benefit June

I initially knew the Anger Makeover is very good for people when they're in conflicts and limiting themselves to their reserved behaviors. When they're trying to act reasonably rather than let out their outspoken behaviors, they often end up hiding their anger and frustration even from themselves. June, like most of us, is at some times and with some people more reserved about negative feelings, and at other times more expressive. At both times for the rest of her life she can use the Anger Makeover to see things more clearly and make good decisions about how to respond.

The Anger Makeover is excellent for times when people are usually sweet and nice. That's the way June carries herself at work. "I avoid confrontations," she admits. "They scare me." This fear of conflict sometimes keeps her anger below the surface. That's not all bad, but then she doesn't know what to do with the frustration. Yes, sometimes she may blurt out the wrong thing and make things worse, but when she didn't have the Anger Makeover, most of the time she didn't know what to say, so she didn't say anything. Sometimes that's not good.

She still isn't always clear about what's going on inside her, or where she stands on an issue. So she's prone to leave herself in the dark, and people around her too. They may wonder, "What is June thinking? How is she feeling about this? Is something wrong?" But usually they go off thinking, "Well, I guess every-thing's fine," even though they sense the brooding. They don't get the benefit of a lighter mood in her, let alone clear, well-exp-ressed ideas from her about the conflict, or see her preferences, viewpoints, or beliefs. Keeping a puzzled, resentful silence can be a sort of hurtful, passive weapon. And then even she doesn't know where she stands, let alone that the world is poorer for missing her viewpoint.

Don't get me wrong. June's ability to hold in her angry feelings is a good trait. It's an ability everybody in the world needs to practice at times. She knows how inappropriate and ineffective people are who are always sounding off, and she has many friends who like and admire her for her ability to stay even-tempered, at least most of the time. The problem is she doesn't know she's missing a vast array of additional appropriate options besides just shutting up. She also misses the powerful benefits from just exploring her feelings, even if she never discusses them with the offending party. She doesn't recognize her own importance. It doesn't occur to her to listen to herself first. It's still important to listen to the other person, but for her maybe this should come later, right after she's listened to herself.

People who usually lead with their quiet side sometimes need practice putting themselves first. Otherwise, they run the risk of routinely getting back at people unconsciously. My friend Peter is usually not an outspoken person, and he sketched this terrible problem of unconscious anger and aggression. "You've seen people like me and my parents," he laughed. "We turn it all in and pretend everything's all right—but then break that special vase by accident, or forget to mail out that bill.

"I get my jollies," Peter explains with a knowing if embarrassed nod, "but not in a constructive way. It's not conscious. I'm not saying, 'I'm going to break that vase.' I'm not deliberately hiding that envelope."

June probably isn't always as nice as she thinks she is, either. She may need the Anger Makeover more urgently than she realizes. The process was created at first for people like June and me. We more often hate confronting someone and hold back from conflicts.

Okay, How About Candid George:
Can the Anger Makeover Benefit Him?

The process can also be useful for people whose outspoken side is more habitual than their quiet side, people like George. He is a highly creative man about forty, one who easily speaks up and lets people know where he stands, but he's also usually able to monitor his expressiveness. He uses the Anger Makeover to not mess things up by talking too quickly.

Yes, The Anger Makeover Can Benefit George

"It helps me wait," he said. "Then I can think it through and decide how to say it so the other person isn't hurt—so they're safe." He laughed, "Even if I think they're obnoxious."

No-Restraints Cliff: Can the Anger Makeover Benefit Him?

Some aggressive people first need to *want* restraint, before they can choose to learn it. It's also true before they even attempt the Anger Makeover—because in this process you go into the anger to learn from it. You need the ability to stand back enough from the anger to go into it without letting it keep catching you. Cliff is an example of someone who probably wouldn't get much from this book—or care. He's a wiry fifty-year-old with frizzy red hair and a hawk-like face. I used to see him occasionally at one of my places of work, and he would ask me about the book I was writing. I told him, "It's an anger book for us ordinary people, especially ones who clam up around anger."

"I don't have that problem," he responded plainly. His voice is a little hard, like slightly rusting iron. "I say whatever I feel. Nobody likes me, and I don't have any friends," he adds, "but that's the way I am."

Just like that. He excused his runaway-mouth habit by declaring it an unchangeable trait. The part about people not liking him was at least partly true. A secretary confided that she couldn't stand him. She remembered him continuing to demand angrily that she get him his medical insurance information, even though she had already explained that she wasn't authorized to do so. I wasn't eager to spend much time with him, though he seemed to get along with some people at a surface level, and I appreciated that he would ask me about my book. That felt good, but even his response to my writing seemed a cynical jab at himself and "the people around here."

"Well," he said, "it'd be good if someone around here made it big." He commented that he and his other coworkers were no-bodies. He mostly griped about the job. Over and over, he would say, "I hate it, I hate it, I hate it." Even his wry humor had a tone of bitterness. Every day seemed to be a bad day for him. This is someone who probably would never read this book. He seemed set in his cynicism because he liked cynicism. He didn't want to change, even though he didn't seem happy. He seemed intelligent enough and could be friendly in his "Isn't it a dumb world" sort of way; but Cliff saw his life as set in stone.

No, Maybe the Anger Makeover Won't Benefit Cliff at Present

To make use of this book, Cliff would need to become interested in changing. My guess is that until he experiences the pain from his shallow habit of gripes and abrasive encounters, he would not have much interest in a book on self-reflection and personal evolution. The Anger Makeover leads to intimacy with Self, which Cliff was taught to avoid. Next the process may then lead to direct self-expression. He seemed to think himself good at direct self-expression, but he was avoiding it. He was focusing on belittling himself and others, staying on the surface, and randomly spewing irritation.

If Cliff ever heard some wake-up call that prompted a strong decision to change, his task would still be tough: to stop his barbs at himself and the people around him, then to take control of his impulse to "just get it off his chest" and sound off about things. Before he could learn from this book on self-awareness leading toward self-expression, he might need to learn more about self-control, slowing down, talking less, listening more, and putting a little emphasis on others' rights and not just his own.

A single use of the Anger-Makeover process can change how we approach an interaction. That may be a miracle in itself, but it may not get us to operate differently in the long term. That's not how we change deeply ingrained conflict habits or handle built-in knee-jerk reactions. Brain and behavior experts (Trafton et al. 2019) said that making real change normally involves the need to reinstate the behavior multiple times. Lapses and relapses are a normal part of the process of achieving positive health habits, just as they are part of the process of overcoming self-destructive behaviors such as drug dependence (p. 8).

So again, who is the Anger Makeover for? Maybe for you. Maybe you wish to keep yourself and others stress-free and fully radiant. Maybe you want to avoid irresponsible overt reactions. Perhaps you want to flip your hidden impulses and turn them into responsible inner power and possible outer communications. Perhaps you wish for honest engagement with those you love or miss. And perhaps you feel impulses similar to those of June, or George. If so, take a breath, and accept this Anger-Makeover challenge. Learn to regularly appreciate impulses and transform them into precious human capabilities.

Power

No One Has Yours

Being Kind, Not Abrupt, Not Distant

Power Is Complex

Power takes many forms, some good for us, some bad for us. Personal power alone is complex enough, but it is the first thing we need to master, so let's discuss it.

Your Definition of Personal Power

What comes to mind when you think of the word power?

In your journal or in the space at the top of the next page, please draw an image that comes to you for the word "power," or write what the word suggests to you at this point, or what you've felt or seen.

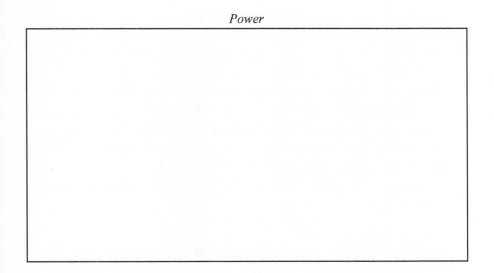

Old Definitions of Power

Often when people think of power, they think of it being abused, and so they not only shy away from anger, they shy away from power as well. We can free ourselves from the age-old confusion between power and malicious behavior. Yes, unscrupulous people need to stop abusing power. And ordinary people all over the globe need to grab hold of their natural, beneficial power.

The following is for people who see harmful uses of power and hesitate to speak up for themselves. If that's not you, hang tight. The Anger Makeover offers crucial insight on gentle, personal power and its effective use.

1. Sometimes the mild-mannered person avoids power. We think power means dominating or forcing someone. So we're afraid to speak up. We hate the thought of controlling people. We know how deeply people resent someone making them do things.
2. Some avoid power because they think it's an all-or-nothing game: "It's me or them." They think setting limits would take away their children's power, so they don't set limits. Or they think it's either-or: I care for myself or for others. So because I love my spouse, I neglect my own wishes.

3. Some think of power as abuse. I've seen how power corrupts, so to keep my integrity, I'll refuse the promotion.
4. Some have felt blame. Misused power is frequently an "It's-all-your-fault" syndrome, so they keep their mouth shut for fear of condemning a friend as bad, or ruining the friend's day, or stirring up the friend's hostility or combativeness. They don't know the alternative. Instead of blaming or making someone wrong, they can request a change in what the person is doing.

Many of us run away from power—at least overt power. It feels better to leave power out of the picture, or at least keep it invisible. It's good to reject abusive power, but we can learn to accept and skillfully use the real power that is ours naturally.

It's not in our nature to be powerless. We inherently have power by being unique.

If we keep ducking direct, active honesty about our unique perspective, our behavior can change in unhelpful ways.

After all, if we say, "Forget power, life is easier without it," we just drive our solid, assertive side underground. If we've run away from power, our brain says, "Well, that's over!" But our soul feels incomplete.

For someone avoiding the power of self-knowledge and self-expression, life at the surface level may appear tranquil and harmonious. Smiles and gentility may abound, but the tranquility feels temporary. By going along with the crowd, we avoid notice for the moment. But inside, we don't feel validated. We didn't add our possible wisdom to an issue that is important to us. At a surface level, we believe this is how life is supposed to be. It's how we can be the popular, caring person we were meant to be. The problem is, if that makes us ditch our power, we may only think we're safe. Depending on the issue or on the relationship, our responsibility may still be there, waiting for us to take it, along with our personal right to occupy our place in the world. Our influence is inborn. Our power is in who we are.

Even the sweetest, most accommodating babies let us know what they want: They fuss when they're wet or sick. It's not in our nature to be powerless. Normally, we know and can promote our interests. We inherently have power by being a unique person with a unique perspective.

As a result, when we duck direct, active honesty, our behavior can change in any number of unhelpful ways. The risk is that some part of us mysteriously launches a sabotage campaign. We're not basically happy and can be uncooperative or unhelpful. We may become silent and stubborn. We exhibit infuriating behaviors, maybe coming late or not showing up. We feel resentful and easily hurt. Some of us cling to control by sniping behind someone's back, causing an increase in frustration and pain. Some feel dominated when a friend says, "I want to lead the group in this direction." Not wanting to dominate in return, they figure they have one course open to them: retreat. But if we abandon our honest identity, people lose sight of us—and don't have the benefit of our thoughts.

A reader commented that although she seldom ducks active honesty, she has unwittingly appeared to launch a campaign by questioning a view. To her, that question seemed muted and innocent, but to her partner, not so innocent. The techniques in this book might help her focus on what she wants and believes in, all while not criticizing or questioning the other person's view. She may find speaking up for her view easier—not in order to convince the other person, but to differentiate, show more of herself, and feel her personal power.

Responsible Power

What is a personal definition of power that gives us a better life? Here is one definition of power that comes up for me. Personal power is "the ability to be and do, using energy from inside me."

Three parts of this definition may help people who are considerate but weak move forward with their growth. First, power is being able to be. It's who we are. Second, this ability extends to doing, whether acting or speaking or simply defining our values for ourselves. We begin by catching on that we already are who we are. Then we can take action, externally or inwardly. Third, we tap the central energy source inside us. In the Anger Makeover, we don't squelch our anger, and we don't give it free reign, especially in its primitive, knee-jerk form. We pay attention to it and find its connection to our preferences and beliefs. That opens us to this central energy source, this "best Self."

Let's feel our way through the three parts of this definition of power to discover what the nature of true power is—and why our anger can lead us to it.

1. By trying on power first as "the ability to be," we can change how we feel physically. It's more internal and personal than "control" or "dominance." Power is a most exciting concept as your personal ability to be yourself.

Your power comes from being in touch with yourself, which this book will help you do. That includes knowing your own perceptions, your position, your preferences, your values and beliefs, the things you accept as a basis for living a good life, all while enjoying a harmonious way of being in the world. You know yourself better at each step and continuously feel yourself developing.

Wilma, a psychotherapist and trainer, said "I was always afraid that if I had too much power people would take me down a notch. So I kept a low profile." She had grown up with two older sisters with special needs. They admired her ability . . . and resented it. They considered her an intrusion and a show-off. Through her infancy, childhood, and youth, they tried to maintain power over her.

After experiencing the Anger Makeover she said, "I see that my ability is about knowing, being, and contributing. It's not about surpassing or alienating other people." She is starting to extend her power as far as it naturally goes, and she's enjoying herself. "My abilities are good for me," she says, "and for others too."

She is regaining her identity and power, recognizing she has full claim, authority, and dominion. Where can we begin this process? By claiming our inner world of knowing, feeling, wanting, and believing. Here is a grip on freedom, maybe our first. Here, inside ourselves, we're less tied to a "power over others" mindset.

Where begin regaining our identity and power? In our inner world of knowing, feeling, wanting, and believing. Here we get our first good grip on freedom. Inside ourselves we're less tied to power over others.

The Anger-Makeover process is designed primarily to help you explore your inner world, to think and define things for yourself. Even in the last step it only asks you to recognize that you have a lot more options than you thought. You need to get a good look at these before you figure out whether or even how to respond to the person triggering your anger reaction. And even if you decide to say or do something, it's very enlightening to imagine it first, inside your head and body, and maybe take a little time out to practice.

At moments when we are feeling more in touch with our timid or passive side, it's a relief to grasp that our first task in conflicts is simply to get a better sense of who we are. If you're prone to self-neglect, there is tremendous power in just embracing the values important to you, underlining the principles you stand for, in yourself, by yourself, and for yourself. Anyone can do it, now and often, and feel like a different person.

The Anger Makeover is a vehicle for discovering and maintaining a vivid picture of your preferences and ideals. Exercising your power with others keeps getting more exciting and less laborious.

2. But personal power is not only the ability to be, it's also the ability to speak or act. True, the Anger Makeover focuses first on straightening out your own thinking, knowing yourself,

and internally embracing your own preferences. But there is more to life than knowing yourself. We sometimes, especially now when there is a national conversation about "allyship" and inclusion of the excluded, we need to speak up and let others know who we are and what we want.

That is power, not domination. People may not immediately buy in to your suggestions, but they benefit from your opening up and simply letting them in on what you honestly know, think, or consider important. Your individual wisdom and perspective are a unique contribution.

What is often needed in conflicts is for the silent to speak up and for the less inhibited to fight the impulse to react too quickly. Is there a way to break our old habits of silence or of noise? There is, if each of us remembers that at our best we are not a bulldozer, but a synthesis of strength, skill, and goodness. You can read more about these three aspects of power in the next section, as a young man named Jason discovers them.

You don't have to adopt your Uncle Jack's biting sarcasm. You don't have to take on a neighbor's habit of in-your-face shouting at her family. You can simply be straightforward in an awake and considerate way and let other people be honest in return. Conflicts are a time to stop and fight the impulse to react too quickly, a time to listen with respect and give others a chance to listen to you with respect.

3. The energy for the power we express has to come from within us. It's a little tricky because, as we've all experienced, we get different kinds of power from different inner parts. Often it's mostly impulse, so the hardest part is to learn to check: How close am I sticking to my most central self? At this moment, am I drawing on the best energy source inside me? Some of us are less attuned to our preferences and values because we've traditionally worried only about other people's. Maybe we just grew up that way, but it has hazards. It often generates a vicious cycle. By not respecting your own gyroscope and spiritual compass, you pass up good chances to speak up for yourself

with personal power. That means less listening to yourself. If you let your inner values get covered over, you have less grip on your power, which is a huge loss. So you come full circle, with even less ability to respect your own gyroscope or spiritual compass.

Anger often comes from thinking someone is trampling on a value close to your center. Maybe that's why the anger can lead you back to an energy source close to your center. At the same time, the stress of the moment can cut you off from your calm and empathy. It has blinded me at times, as it has most people I know. Once you get back to your center, you can exert power with less strain or tension. The Anger Makeover uses anger to tap back into your inner center, your Self, and feel the heart energy in that source. This is the energy you then channel into action. True power is awesome. It involves directing this strong energy, but with skill and caring.

You direct it the way you direct one of those power mowers that you ride. A power mower can take a misguided person through the middle of the tulips, but a little practice and making the choice to direct the mower skillfully and harmlessly can get the job done.

In some situations, we tend to be overly "caring" for fear of messing up love and mutual respect. We're afraid to take power, but true power increases love and mutual respect: We're caring for ourselves—and, surprisingly, others.

Sometimes even drawing from a central inner energy source isn't enough, because both people in a conversation need to do that. We've all experienced how people often resist honest, caring exchange when a difference arises.

Granted, some will not join us in a caring, honest exchange that preserves mutual respect. We start with those who will.

But we can encourage heartfelt interaction. And we can start with those who *will* join us in respectfully finding commonalities and defining authentic differences. It is a problem that right now those people seem few and far between, but that's why I want us to start with people with whom we already have a significant enough relationship. Otherwise, what's the point of talking? The purpose of the discussion must be the first question. If you don't decide together on your purpose, there is no point except argumentation. Arguments seldom go anywhere. When's the last time someone convinced you in an argument? If the purpose is to prove I'm right or to show the flaws in the other person's thinking, no one has power. It takes two to turn an argument into a discussion, but it only takes one to suggest it. If the purpose is not about respect and discovering each other's cherished values, we first need to agree on some other mutually acceptable purpose. Without it, there's little hope that anyone will be looking inside and drawing from an inner source of energy, a source more central than their irritable reaction.

The goal, then, has to do with mutual respect and discovery. In the Anger-Makeover process, we tap hidden power sources in us by paying attention to our feelings in order to have them lead us to discovering and honoring submerged values all our own. That plugs us in to the dynamo of the self. That is an exciting connection, because this true self is something more than the rudderless selves people live in more than half the time. If we ignore or forever suppress our feelings, whether negative or positive, we lose a valuable path to self-direction. There is no internal control or guidance. Taking back our identity by embracing our unique values gives us unbelievable, effortless, unique power.

My client Kara says, "Not only do our values give us power to think for ourselves, they give us power to actually do or take action." For example, she says that in the gardening world we can get an immense amount of work done just by riding a mower. In the world of people, we accomplish remarkable results riding the energy of our values, rather than our positions, which tend to get us defensive or offensive. I go into the difference in a later section. With much less effort, we're speaking up for ourselves directly and respectfully.

That is exactly what the Anger-Makeover process is designed for: finding and embracing the relevant values inside us .

Stepping Into Power: An Example

A client named Jason came to me saying he was stalled in life. He was 23. We discovered that he had been avoiding his anger because he understandably thought of it as distorted power. I wanted him to find and feel good about his power, and told him he could have healthy, shared power. I told him that effective use of your will is a synthesis of three qualities that we all have. This was wisdom from Robert Assagioli, who taught that the three qualities of a healthy will are strength, goodness, and skill. I asked Jason what he thought: Could expressing himself with a combination of these three qualities bring him power he could welcome into his life?

It turned out that Jason had also held back from striking out on his own in life for fear of hurting his parents' feelings. He had always thought they would be disappointed if he didn't become a lawyer like his father, who had become a district judge, or at least study business administration. His anger at them and their vision of him had shut down his spirit. He had never given himself the freedom to wonder seriously what he wanted to do. Even though he had financial support for whatever educational path he wanted to pursue, he couldn't let his own purpose emerge from inside himself.

By his junior year in a pre-law track in college, he was feeling extremely pressured and despondent. His grades were bad, but he didn't want to drop the effort. He was afraid it would be mean to veer off from what he thought his parents expected.

His parents had apparently not ever known how to listen to him. Nor had he known how to speak directly to them and still be a good person and a respectful son. He said he was starting to wish he could go to sleep and not wake up. Surprising even himself, he had taken a whole bottle of aspirin.

The school provided Jason counseling which he used briefly, and he managed to finish college. He started working toward an

MBA, still trying to stay in his parents' ballpark. He came to me near the end of his first year in graduate school, frustrated and again depressed. In my first session with Jason it was clear to me that he had come to a decision. He wanted to be more honest and powerful with his parents. He knew he had to learn to stand up for himself—and let them know he was not going to do what they wanted.

But he was still stumped. Because of the pent-up anger he felt, he was afraid he would have to unleash his feelings on his parents. He thought anything he'd say would wound them. Worse, he'd end up with his parents mad at him.

He was confusing power with abuse, control, and blame, as have many people since civilization began.

He thought it was a win-lose problem: If he won, he would be making his parents lose. He dreaded having to hurt them and risk losing their love and friendship. That was a real risk, because his idea of power had always been that you have to hit back hard, so he had long resisted it. Like many who have been trying for many years to be sweet and nice, he knew he had to change something. Like many of us, he thought he had to become his opposite. Like many, he was afraid that to save himself he had to risk damaging others, even loved ones.

Power: The Synthesis of Strong, Good, and Skillful

In our second session, as we talked about how to access and use the three important qualities of true power, he began to appear energized. This was a new picture. He hadn't thought of a new style including strength, goodness, and skill all at once. I was reassuring him that if he was going to begin expressing himself effectively, he would need all three.

I told him about the Anger Makeover. He could take it with him in his head and use it every time he felt hurt or angry. I encouraged him to stop playing down his own feelings. It's like magic. People can turn sadness and frustration into feelings of connection and power. Here, in a nutshell, are the three ingredients of the new plan I offered Jason for self-expression.

46

Strong Will: First, I told him he could be decisive and strong with his parents without having to become obnoxious or mean. Once you know your position and what you want to say, you can move forward persistently, patiently and with strength. Strength is one aspect of power. In his book *The Act of Will,* Assagioli calls it "strong will." The Anger Makeover might help Jason become firmer and more self-assured. He would need courage and nerve to behave in a new way and stick with it. However, toughness or will power alone would not take him from his anger to real power.

Good Will: Second, along with firmness, I told him, you'll need reverence, respect. Can someone show respect, and even give praise, while expressing anger? Yes, if the anger has had a make-over. It's my idea of what Assagioli calls "good will." Yes, you will indeed need to start speaking up with your parents, but you can do it with love. You need to *keep* that quality of caring you have always had for them and everyone else. Jason could continue being considerate while improving his self-expression.

He was smiling and nodding, more alive than I had seen him. Yes, he was proud of who he was. "I've always cared a lot about people." He was seeing that I didn't expect him to tell off his parents. He did not have to ignore them. He did not have to withdraw from them.

You always will be a caring person, I asserted. You don't ever have to give that up. He knew he didn't want to become selfish and hard. But he had thought it was either-or: care about others, or care about himself. He had been sacrificing himself for others. No one had shown him how to develop a synthesis of self-care along with caring for others.

Skillful Will: Third, I cautioned him not to swing from hesitancy to the other extreme, believing every impulse. Maintaining conscious purpose and being shrewd is an aspect of power Assagioli called "skillful will." To speak up for himself effectively, Jason would have to stay alert and resourceful. Timing, humor, and finesse are natural allies of responsible power. By taking time to use your head, you can act consciously. You don't have to delay encounters by contemplating endlessly, as many of us overly thoughtful people keep doing. You lose your opportunity if you wait too long or rush in without a clear purpose.

In fact, you can't make the combination of strength and goodness work unless you maintain a shrewd sense of your real purpose. Purpose is the positive things you want to accomplish by your behavior. It's not revenge or putting people in their place. Happily, having a positive purpose opens an infinite pool of creative ways to accomplish it.

Jason was starting to foresee self-expression as a creative combination of his new, self-caring honesty and his old caring for others. Caring came naturally and was precious to him. Already a loving person, he proceeded to pull together his strength, goodness, and skill into a new style and go from anger to power.

Yes, Change the World: Start at Home

In the real world, we need power to be ongoing and mutual. It's not some wronged, brutal hero in a movie rising stealthily and launching a single shell across the ravine, exploding the evil enemy into a million bits. Rather, we must regularly choose what to say about what we see and feel while still honoring the friend or loved one's position, or at least the person's good intention.

The only true power is shared power. The survival mechanism in our brain repeatedly whispers sharply that a loved one who doesn't agree with our view must be the enemy. It's hardly likely. We do not want them to disappear and not be constant contributors to our lives. We are all sure we're right, but no one has a monopoly on the truth.

Each of us throughout life is creating a sort of personal library of world information and principles for living. We benefit whenever we accept other people's books into our library. Every person's viewpoint is unique and a valuable contribution. By making sure we include our viewpoint as well as the other person's, we create a new spark. We're rubbing together different positive perspectives. That gives us a new reality, a synthesis. It's not argument. It's not bland compliance.

My niece says, "Honestly, isn't it often going to be you doing more of the work, dealing with others' reactions, unless you have an unbelievably amiable and chill set of relationships?" She's right. Whether to get on board is a real choice. And those of us who say yes need to start practicing, practicing, practicing. If we stay on board we will learn as we go. As soon as the hundredth monkey gets it, a sea change will occur.

It's combining opposite values that is, if we can find our way to real values, to the element in each that is positive. And the surprise is how easy this can be once the positives in the opposite values are uncovered and combined. We can even bring each other's values to

Well, we're right! Of course. We know it. But no one has a monopoly on the truth.

Everyone is carefully creating a personal library of information and principles for living—everyone, not just us. It benefits us to slip into our library helpful "books" from other people's libraries—other unique, precious additions to our viewpoints.

fullness by working on them together. It may not happen overnight, and both parties may have to allow time before they can acknowledge the underlying values on both sides. Even friends, lovers, and coworkers have to come out of their respective silos at times if they want to support and clarify each other's values. Granted, it seems to be a new skill; we may be evolving to a new stage of development and may never be the same.

That is a tip. Search for positive values. It helps this synthesis process work. My friend Isabelle, a Swiss writer and educator, learned about synthesis studying with Assagioli himself. She said that in the process of synthesis, each of the parts remains complete in itself even as the parts come together. In fact, for synthesis to happen, the parts have to reach perfection. This tells me that when we have day-to-day differences with coworkers and partners, we need the exact opposite of trying to tear down each other's arguments. Not only do we need to support each other's right to have opposite visions, we need to help bring the visions to perfection. That's impossible, unless we maintain respect and gentleness.

Who has the time and energy for that? It's your choice how much time and energy you spend with a given incident, but the end result, the prize, may well be worth your decision to stop and find the time and energy. The resulting synthesis is something distinctly new. It is far bigger than the sum of the parts. We're participating in evolution. We're building. We're leaving the world better than we found it—and ending up with enriched relationships to boot.

Meanwhile, all parties are gaining positive personal power. All are included. All participate. Colleagues and loved ones are always quite different from each other and prize the information they have to exchange. The exchange takes bravery, but it's exhilarating. All feel a return of energy and vitality, healing and renewal. This spreads outward to their communities and the world. So, to solve the mess the world's in we must start at home and at work, in our familiar, love-filled corners of the mess. You're not just listening; you're also speaking up for yourself with strength, goodness, and skill. Listening is the most crucial and difficult step for people who favor their expressive side. Speaking up with care is the most crucial and difficult step for people who favor their reserved side.

No wonder my vision includes experimenting with small stuff to learn this. We must pause, repeatedly. Leaving a vast world of politics on the shelf for a bit, we first settle in to apply the Anger-Makeover process in our very local world of person-to-person interactions. While we're still novices, there's a benefit to not immediately trying to use the process to wrestle down our full-strength reactions to politicians and events. We have a better chance at not getting sidetracked from our learning. It's easy to get drawn in and let conflicts about oversized national and international issues and intense moral convictions overpower our good will. We need to maintain good will as we gain inner power.

If we're routinely in front of the TV going into fight-or-flight mode, feeling powerless, or succumbing to hating some opposing politician or position, we may need to put in some time and work on ourselves. Once we've had a little success with the Anger Makeover on easier issues at work and at home, *then* we could experiment with gaining positive personal power with politics. And good luck. Even then, we'll need to take note repeatedly of our urges. For example, we refrain from putting down that idiot or that distortion when we could be redefining and marinating in our preferences, strengths, and values.

The choice is ours. We can put someone else down, or pull ourselves up—and maybe the other person. We may feel compelled to correct something a friend is wrong about; or we might change course and pause and say what we'd like, or pause and correct our style or strategy. We might go inside to where our body feels the angry reaction, where there is always a specific underlying, constructive value, something deeper down that at that moment we're passionately protecting or cherishing, and find the power source under the angry feelings and opinions. The first task is already a handful, to remember to pause so we can use the Anger Makeover to transform our own reactions. But it's easier if we start with our less-angry reactions with colleagues, friends, and loved ones. That transformation task is more doable.

Yes, even the reactions that hit us at home and work may feel completely daunting. So let me dial this guidance down lower. Say we start with only easy irritation reactions at home and work, and build our power gradually. We pick our battles, or rather, our peaceful efforts to differentiate. We limit ourselves to respectfully stating one or two preferences or positive values. We start with the easy differences, but whenever possible with an eye to putting the opposite energies together into new combinations. While we're at it, imagine making that a joint effort with the colleague or loved one.

Here's a bit of encouragement, not just for you, but for me too. Even if a relationship gets torn, and even if we can't revitalize it, we can always take time to improve our own differentiation tools, immediately and for the future. Every time we make the effort and get past being stuck, every time we practice converting our own anger into constructive energy, every time we pick up our part of the burden and aim at having a two-way connection, we're making a bridge over a space between us and our partner. We all need to keep practicing.

Even in our personal day-to-day world, war is too common. War is not personal power, it's impersonal power. In fact, even little wars at work and home make us lose our personal power—and we miss out on practicing valuable peaceful conflict. It's a natural tendency. Even as colleagues or couples, we grab for weapons such as debunking a position, giving the cold shoulder, exploiting a weak spot, or making an accusation. Better to reach for tools such as asking the other to say more; listening with curiosity and interest; helping each other clarify our meaning; or naming the values each of us seems to be espousing. That calls for speaking up respectfully and courageously.

Otherwise, even these homegrown wars cause a jumble of trouble. Defensive self-justification brings more argument, along with hurt, walls, grief, wasted energy, hopelessness, demand for perfection, loss of love and respect. The remedy? Not necessarily just being silent, because silence can also be a wall. Yes, we need silence, but introduced with words like "Let me think about this." And after using the silence constructively, by applying steps from the Anger-Makeover process, we may be able to offer a gift, such as strong, humble conflict, respectful listening, and our words that make explicit not only respect for the colleague or loved one, but also respect for ourselves and our feelings. And we can always practice carefully combining our reserved and expressive skills. While that takes personal power, it has the potential to spark solutions never seen before.

Now What's Your Personal Definition of Power?

In this Section, you've heard my ideas about power. Perhaps you were thinking for yourself and getting new ideas, hopes, or inspirations. At this moment, what would you say real power is for you? What is settling out in you from all this?

In your journal or in the space below, draw or write what your picture of power is now, or scribble a working definition of the kind of power you'd like:

You might write something as simple as "My unique ability," or as full as "Being able to make choices jointly by honoring my and another person's vision." Maybe it's "repeatedly drawing on inner purpose with inner strength, goodness, and skill to accomplish something I value," or "ability to make choices jointly and act." I'd love to know your ideas and successes, what you think integrated power is, and how you think it might work for you.

The P-O-W-E-R Worksheet

Five Anger Makeover Steps

What follows is a quick worksheet that's the heart of an internal process of five steps. Don't worry: The Anger-Makeover process doesn't tell you whether to say or do anything with the other person. It prepares you to choose for yourself what to say or not say or do. These steps are inner work. They're easy to learn. Try them. Take them for a spin. See how you change inside, what you learn, what questions arise. Later in the book we'll be walking you through them in more detail.

For now, I suggest you just pick an issue you feel frustrated about and go quickly through the process. The five steps let you think through uncomfortable inner reactions, the reflexes your brain immediately created inside about the issue outside you. For now, you're just doing inward-focused work. Later you can use the results to decide whether to speak or act, or what to say or do, and for what purpose.

You can simply write a phrase or a sentence for each of the five steps. Sometimes after two steps you already see your way forward, but I suggest you write on all five before you stop. That expands your inner response to the issue and usually gives you ready-made outer responses. Once you are feeling more relaxed and calmer, you may be glad you wrote down your thoughts.

The worksheet on pages 56 and 57 lets you try out the process and gives you written notes. I encourage you to make several copies of the worksheet and keep copies on hand, ready for you to repeat the process when you notice other issues coming up.

Notice the word "repeat" at the top of the worksheet. It's not enough to have the information about how important it is to sweeten how you interact in conflicts. Motivation is vital, but "information alone is rarely sufficient to meaningfully alter behavior," say Trafton et al. (p. 9). They go on: "Information about why to change a behavior may be necessary to motivate change, but practice and support for new behaviors are needed to create enduring health-related habits." That's why for my purposes I copy the worksheet and repeat, repeat, repeat with lots of little conflicts, over lots of time. Practice builds expanded consciousness and new habits.

Select an issue now, try out a worksheet, and make note of any questions that come up. You may find the answers on pages 93 through 180. Those sections give guidance, first on the process as a whole and then on each step.

The Anger-Makeover process can radically transform how you feel, and you can try it out right now.

P-O-W-E-R Worksheet

*Make Copies of This Worksheet. Fill in the spaces. **Repeat.***

Name a problem that irritates or concerns you.

```
┌─────────────────────────────────────────────────┐
│                                                 │
│                                                 │
│                                                 │
│                                                 │
│                                                 │
└─────────────────────────────────────────────────┘
```

Picture the Problem

Describe the specific words and actions. Tell what a video would show, and the possible harm done. **Examples**: *"He was doing 55 in a 35-mph zone. He cut me off." "That is scary. And it could cause accidents."*

```
┌─────────────────────────────────────────────────┐
│                                                 │
│                                                 │
│                                                 │
│                                                 │
│                                                 │
└─────────────────────────────────────────────────┘
```

Own Your Own Feelings, in Your Body and Emotions

Instead of blaming or name-calling (outward focus on the person or event), write your physical and emotional reactions to the problem, such as mad, sad, glad, scared, or hurt. **Examples**: *"I feel like yelling. Frustrated. Grateful we're all okay. Angry. My heart hurts. Afraid, shaking. Strong energy in my fists and shoulders. Sad."*

```
┌─────────────────────────────────────────────────┐
│                                                 │
│                                                 │
│                                                 │
│                                                 │
│                                                 │
└─────────────────────────────────────────────────┘
```

Want What *You* Want. Be Specific

Write what you'd have *preferred* in place of what the person said or did—also possible benefits. **Examples**: *"I would prefer she drive slower, stay in one lane, keep some distance. That could reduce tension, accidents."*

```




```

Enjoy and Embrace Your Values

Write the qualities and *values* of yours that make you want those changes. **Examples**: *"I care about safety. I think things go better when people drive carefully and keep a cushion of distance."*

```




```

Review Your Range of Options

List things you could say or do. **Examples**: *Ideas from your responses above. Other insights, feelings, and beliefs. Options ranging from reserved to expressive.* "I can keep calm, drive slower, stay at a safe distance. I can voice my preference *for specific safe-driving practices."*

```




```

This *inner* work sets you up to decide on creative outer words/actions. You can respectfully show your unique self, your personal power (your unique ability to be and do, guided from within).

To explore what you are grasping and clear your head for what's to come, please use space in your journal or below to draw what you're seeing. Or do some stream-of-consciousness writing, or try some scribbled ranting for your eyes only:

The Anger Makeover
in Relationships

Here are two live examples: anger at a spouse, and anger at yourself. Later we'll walk through each Anger-Makeover step and offer suggestions.

Example 1: Using the Anger Makeover to Transform
Anger at a Spouse

This first story highlights the effectiveness of the first four Anger-Makeover steps as a simple progression that changed a client. "I feel good," she said, "like I have something new to offer the other person. I'm not helpless and angry and disappointed with myself." People use the Anger Makeover to help themselves—and avoid arguing, giving someone the cold shoulder, or being sarcastic. They get new, effective ideas.

If the following issue seems trivial, remember that people's internal reactions to seemingly small issues can feel intense, immense, and immovable. They destroy relationships. As I've suggested in earlier sections, it may be easier for us today to make smaller, doable changes, ones that improve our personal relationships. Later, if we keep practicing—and practice we must—we may feel more hope about changing our reactions to politicians and deep moral problems. If we enjoy success practicing on our smaller reactions, then later we can start changing tough old political habits such as disgust with the other party, soaking in resentment, being overcome by outrage, and indulging in judgments.

Ana Maria's Story

I worked with a woman in her early thirties headed toward divorce. She came in for her third session looking rather pale and tired, with lines under her eyes. After two weeks separated from her husband James, she was feeling lonely and isolated. Close to tears, she didn't want to "open that book"—let the dam of emotions overflow. She was afraid she couldn't even function, especially at work. "I feel like I'm riding out a storm," she said, "letting a little time go by."

Her biggest concern was that her husband was now "sliding off the agreement" to get the divorce. Now he thought the divorce a wrong move. "I'm wondering," she said, "didn't I get through to him about how miserable I am?"

The dilemma was what to do next. "Do I try to tell him how miserable I am with him—and feel like a mean person? Or do I keep it all bottled up? That's what I do all the time. Then later I end up exploding anyway."

Has any of us not been in a similar dilemma?

Would the Anger Makeover benefit this person? I thought it might help her with self-care in the relationship. "Can you tell your husband what he's been doing that hurts you?"

"I can't tell him." Her knuckle was at her mouth. "I always remember my dad criticizing me as a little girl. I'd make a mistake, and he'd scold and drill me. I felt so humiliated." Yes, she was using her reserved side more than her expressive side, and the Anger-Makeover process might coach her in exploring her expressive skills without fear of blowing up at her husband. With her husband, she was too accustomed to being passive. To shutting up, picking up her marbles and going home. Leaving. Withdrawing.

And the Anger Makeover could also have helped if she had been mostly using her expressive side, by helping her limit the expression to preferences and values, and avoiding and judgments.

I wanted Ana Maria to grasp other options besides bottling up her irritation and "blowing up later." She needed to start the process of clear differentiation. She wouldn't be able to define herself well until she released tension through finding her preferences, embracing her values, and feeling the calm and strength of her more-centered self.

The Anger-Makeover process emphasizes preferences. A misguided "me-first" attitude often turns preferences into demands.

Right now, it seemed that when she was with her husband she was not only not clearly differentiated, she didn't even feel fully human. The Anger Makeover could help her find her underlying values and personality. The reptilian brain is naturally reactive—in fact, overly reactive. Even though overreactions have protected our safety and integrity since ancient times, they are still overreactions. But our overreactions are unique to each of us. How we overreact depends on our life experience. I didn't want to brand as wrong Ana Maria's more fearful than angry style, her flight or freeze overreactions to her husband's behavior. Helping her notice her passive overreactions could be the first step toward basking in the pristine values underlying them. Once she felt safe and intact in more stable inner territory, she might move forward instead of staying gripped by overreactions.

Overreactions are ordinary, day-to-day versions of fight, flight, freeze, or fawn. Ana Maria's were getting her in trouble, whereas responding from her underlying, unique values might help her. Your values don't necessarily exclude other peoples' values. People's very different preferences can be complementary—they may be opposite but they don't have to abolish each other.

I wouldn't try to stymie or "correct" Ana Maria's exasperation, but help her stay with it and take it deeper, to the underlying values and truths. At that deeper level of intrinsic worth, which she seemed not to be feeling, her values might complement her husband's, so maybe synthesis would be possible. Synthesis enables creative new worlds of collaboration and cooperation to evolve. Synthesis isn't going to result if you try to become less aggressive by being more passive. For Ana Maria, inner synthesis might flourish if she let go of aggressive and passive weapons and started to develop combinations of reserved and expressive communication tools.

It helps if we can teach ourselves and our clients to notice our reptilian brains' repeated moments of instant irritation, and immediately smile at them with gratitude. They are doing their typical, faithful work of overreacting. Gratitude lets us relax. Then we can move on toward synthesis by embracing the solid principles that the overreactions are trying to safeguard. Reptilian or lizard brain is not a demeaning term. It's a realistic one. And we must be grateful for the consistent, automatic, reptile-like guardianship we get from that part of our brain. We can then identify with the part of us that is more than the overreactions, smiling and forging on toward warm principles and synthesis.

Ana Maria's Impasse and Failed Approach

Ana Maria was in a quandary. She thought it would be inconsiderate and dangerous to sit her husband down and get more real about how unhappy she had been with him. She wasn't afraid of him but of herself—she would judge, criticize, or try to fix him.

"If you talked with him," I asked, "could you give him specific examples?"

"Okay. I'd probably say, 'James, you never think. You just can't. You're always screwing up, and it disgusts me."

She could benefit from Step One of the Anger Makeover: focus on *specific behavior*. She was generalizing and assuming he couldn't think. Seeing him as forever defective is the definition of hopelessness. Was he incapable of behaving some other way, or was he behaving out of habit, or self-defense?

"It absolutely drives me crazy," she said. "I know I should

accept him unconditionally, but it's inexcusable." Had that shriek of criticism within her own mind been making things worse, helping him define himself as a hopeless case, locking in his mistakes? She needed a constructive purpose, to get clear about her own position, eventually even suggest more appropriate behavior to him. The Anger Makeover might help Ana Maria's thinking become more self-affirming and constructive.

Maybe she could learn to see her criticisms as preferences and voice them as requests and specific suggestions. Maybe she could put them in a more caring context, such as, "I love you, and I like when you do such-and-such. Can we make a deal on a change in this behavior here?" She wasn't getting clear about specific behaviors of his. Instead, she was mentally rehearsing personal attacks, as you and I may tend to do. Maybe her telling herself James "always" screws up and "never" thinks had helped her put this manageable difference on the road to divorce.

She said, "We do fine in many other areas." They traveled well together. Both liked romantic weekends together and were attracted to each other. They tried to be kind to each other. Still, for years their relationship had been getting marred by times of extreme exasperation and hopelessness, because his mushy thinking clashed with her expectations of precise, careful thought, and because she wanted to be seen clearly for who she was. Fortunately, neither of them had added the huge complication of affairs. Wasn't it a shame for them to be ending their marriage over his failure to "see" her, which she felt was happening all the time. Why had she let it keep happening? "I want to say something, but any time I criticize someone, I feel like the bad guy."

Could the Anger Makeover help Ana Maria start with herself and replace her old way of thinking? Up to now, her thinking had been a mix: the generalities of always and never, feeling sure he really couldn't change, being afraid she couldn't say anything without hurting or angering him, thinking she had to hold her anger down and minimize the central problem of him not seeing the real her. The simple Anger-Makeover steps seemed ideal and might take her in a whole new direction.

These steps are a useful way to think about our anger and

clear our minds. Then, instead of being stopped up, the anger becomes much easier to talk about in a way that invites exchange. Let's look at the new thinking Ana Maria needed in order to understand her anger in a way that validates her inborn power.

New P-O-W-E-R Thinking

"Let me give you a tool," I said, "to get you out of this dilemma of either being a demon or shutting up. There may be new options for what to say to James. Maybe you're still deciding whether to talk to him about your irritation. You can face that decision after you think this situation through from a new angle."

"Great!" She glanced sharply at me, as if I had been holding out on her. I had been. I was checking. It would have required more caution to try the Anger-Makeover process if she had a hard time controlling her tongue or was prone to explode at James. That didn't seem to be the case; she was afraid to speak up. She sat up straight. This woman who liked to feel competent was ready to learn something new about competency.

1: Focus on Specific Behavior

I told her, "This Anger-Makeover tool uses the word POWER as a memory aid. Five letters for five steps. Instead of being afraid of your anger, you can explore it and use it to find your power, inside you. You find a calm power by going into your anger."

I told her the first step is **P,** for **Picture the Problem.** We start with an accurate description. I asked if she could choose one concrete, observable behavior from among the things she had just been telling me about.

"OK," she said. "When I'm reading a book, I write notes in the margin to highlight quotes I really like. I had seen a quote I loved and had written in the margin, 'Remember this when you need your power.' James came in, found the book lying open, and started reading my note aloud. My handwriting isn't so terrible, but he got as far as 'power' and stumbled. Somehow, he couldn't make out the word and blurted out, 'Powder? Ponder?' He let his mouth get ahead of his brain."

To some it may seem like a very small thing, but not to her. It was a good, specific example of what caused her pain and inner conflict. She already had mentioned her father's demands and criticism of her as a child. Had she internalized perfectionism, irritability, a need to control, and resentment?

And even if it had been just a small misunderstanding and an overreaction on her part—certainly it was a concerning, habitual mistake on his part—small misunderstandings and big overreactions contribute to the 50 percent of American marriages ending in divorce. Overreactions can devastate both people.

I wanted her to apply the Anger Makeover and mentally affirm herself. To experience her calm, confident center. It would start her out with being kind to herself. This would not be a strategy for letting go of the negative to focus on the positive. She would immediately focus on and use the negative feelings and events, and go through them to appreciate her preferences, her positive values, and who she was.

In the next few steps this eye-opening process changed Ana Maria's state of mind and possibly her life. The first four steps give the essential inner movement.

I encouraged Ana Maria to start by writing down her picture of the problem about James's behavior in the space provided under Step One on her worksheet. I suggested eliminating "always," "never," and other judgmental generalities. She should record just his behavior, the specific things he had said or done.

For Step 1, **P: Picture the Problem**, she wrote:

> *James blurted out the wrong word. He got the simple word "power" wrong. It's an important word to me.*

"That was simple!" Ana Maria exclaimed with a puzzled squint, almost as if to add, "a little too simple, maybe?"

"It's simple and clear," I said. She had done a pretty good job of being specific and descriptive, and she had avoided getting caught in some general, screaming judgment inside her, such as,

"He was acting like an idiot." That first external stepping stone of describing words or actions could move her to the next, internally focused step: owning her inner emotions about the external event:

2: Instead of Judging or Criticizing the Other Person, Name *Your Emotions*

So in step one Ana Marie described the external event and avoided getting stuck complaining. This second step looks inward to highlight her emotions. This is not to be confused with the familiar, confusing advice that you've got to let out your feelings, not bottle them up. Number one, that advice gets misinterpreted to mean just voice your knee-jerk anger and accusations, as in, "You're wrong. That's stupid!" Number two, the advice assumes the choices are either to yell or stuff it. There's another alternative: pause and go deeper and consider saying something effective, such as, "I believe in x and would prefer y." Number three, that standard advice assumes it's okay to vent in earshot of other people. Venting angrily is likely to do harm if we don't protect our colleague or loved one. Avoiding that harm might mean ensuring we only vent in private.

In this step I was getting Ana Maria simply to identify her emotions, to name anger, sadness, fear, or hate. An emotion is a specific response you feel in your body

In place of the name-calling, judgment, and criticism I wanted her to experience her emotions—even if she never expressed them to James.

and psyche or soul. I wanted her to realize that she was skimming over her emotions when voicing criticisms or judgments such as "He's so inept" or "He behaves like a clown." I wanted her to define her emotions for herself.

"Now," I said, "let's move to Step Two, **O: Own Your Emotions.** I'm asking you to name the wide-ranging feelings you have about this irritating behavior of James's. Not your judgments or what you *think* about him, but what you feel inside, in your body."

"I was personally disappointed that he didn't recognize the word power."

"It was a personal disappointment," I repeated. This behavior hurt her deeply.

"Yes. I thought, 'James, don't you even know what I am?' I'm a strong person. The power in me says to him, 'What's wrong with you that you can't read, you jerk? You inattentive pea-brain.'"

"How would it feel," I asked, "to leave off the 'jerk' and 'inattentive pea brain' parts and say, 'I feel angry and hurt'?" Even if she never voiced this to James, the focus on giving names to her emotions had put her attention where it belonged. The initial visceral, automatic reaction had triggered an inner scream. It was name-calling, judgment, and criticism. This had been pulling her away from experiencing and voicing her emotions.

"Oh, yes." Her voice was firm. "I feel a lot of anger and hurt. And saying it feels strong and real."

I paused to let her feel it, then went on. "And it sounds like you're feeling the loneliness you've described in past sessions."

"Yes," she agreed. "I feel lonely. I'm right there, and he's not paying attention."

"So, the emotions you're owning in this step are disappointment, anger and hurt, and loneliness."

"Yes," she agreed in soft voice, shaking her head. "Yes." She sighed. Her attention at this point was directed inward. Her eyes were staring at a point behind me, almost as if she were back in that incident, being disappointed all over again.

I helped her get her full list down on paper in the space provided for Step Two. She wrote the following for **O:** Own Your Emotions:

> *Personal disappointment*
> *Anger and hurt*
> *Loneliness*

Writing down your discoveries in each step gives a precise written record, one which can be useful at the end. These written words will keep the energy alive and help focus it toward a useful purpose. You can see this step moving her attention away from the outer scene and more toward her inner world—which is more complex than just her anger impulse.

Looking to see more energy emerge in the following steps, I pushed on.

3: Identify Your Preferences or Wants

Now I asked Ana Maria to state her preferences, what she wanted in place of what James said and did. Step Three, the **W** of **POWER,** stands for **Want the Specific Changes You Sincerely Want.**

She understood immediately. "I'd just want James to take the time to look closely. All he has to do is puzzle it out, and get it right. He puts the burden of interest and correcting on me. He just blurts out lazy thoughts. I want to tell him, 'Do the work yourself: Figure it out for yourself.'"

"It's something so important to you for James to figure it out for himself. You want him to throw himself into understanding and really seeing you." This filled in more of the picture of her issue with her husband. "So you'd prefer if he'd take a real interest in you and put energy into figuring things out for himself."

"Right." Ana Maria was thinking. "Well that's just me..." She seemed to think she was going out on a limb. I was trying to let her know that she was being clear and understandable. "Start with the words, 'I want' or 'I'd prefer,'" I said. She roused herself and didn't back down. She stuck to her point. These preferences seemed important to her.

At this point it's good to ask how this feels. When people are letting go of a suppressed demand, or a yelled demand, especially in situations where they're more expressive, it often feels strange but good, like releasing a clamp on the heart. Expressing wants and preferences is not the usual behavior. Their shoulders relax, their core becomes strong, their world feels more spacious. And this is just the beginning of a forward movement. In the step after this, the experience expands even further when they find and embrace the values underlying these wants.

Ana Maria scribbled her preferences for Step Three, **W: Want the Specific Changes You Want:**

> *I'd prefer that he take a real interest in me.*
> *I want him to figure things out for himself.*

Perhaps for a long time Ana Maria had been confused about her own preferences and had not had a clue how to state them as preferences and not angry demands. The Anger Makeover was proving to be a remedy. She stopped questioning her preferences and began realizing they came from valid irritations and pain. She had been dismissing her frustration saying, "Well that's just me," but the frustration was still tying her in knots. Embracing her preferences resolved the confusion. She would begin to feel the strength and self-reliance available in her core personality. She would be able to replace her habit of silent judgment, which was hurting her husband's feelings and her self-esteem.

Taken by itself, what Ana Maria was saying made good sense. I figured James surely could have taken ten or twenty seconds longer to work it out and say it right. I had little doubt that Ana Maria's handwriting was clear enough. I couldn't know why he kept doing this, nor could I fully grasp why it had led Ana Maria to want a divorce, but the mystery was getting clearer. It would continue becoming clearer in the next step.

4: Enjoy and Embrace Your Values: Principles Underlying Your Wants, Beliefs You Live By

For Anna Maria, what she sincerely wanted led directly to principles important to her.

"It sounds like James's actions go against some deep values of yours," I said. Ana Maria thought his habits were permanent qualities. *In her mind,* his behaviors were "locked in," unchangeable. Her locked-in reactions were part of the problem.

"In Step Three you said that you want James to show self-reliance. So self-reliance is important to you, a quality you believe in," I said. "The next step is the **E** of **POWER, Enjoy and Embrace**

Your Values. Are you ready to look at who *you* are, based on your wants, how your preferences can connect you to your values?"

"Yes," she murmured, her eyes seeming to get bigger.

"It's a strong part of who you are, right?" This was to focus her on just how important a value self-reliance was for her.

"Yes," she shook her head slowly, as if in a dream. "Yes, it is."

"Would you say self-reliance is good for humans generally?"

"Right..." she said tentatively, almost as if she thought this might be carrying things too far. But she seemed to be starting to feel how her values were not just hers, how their connection to the rest of humanity made her stronger.

"You could say, 'Things go better when people show self-reliance."

"Yes!" she said, and pushed on with what seemed an inner, driving energy. "And problem solving, analytical skill—and restraint. When they have the discretion to keep their mouth shut until they've worked through a problem."

"And when they get things right," I added. It seemed a good moment for her to feel solidly braced by all the strong values she had already put into words.

"Right!" She was leaning forward.

"You have your hands on your chest." I pressed both my hands over the middle of my upper chest, just as she was doing—as if her heart was beating hard, or she was holding back a surge of energy. She seemed like a child freed from long anxiety just learning she's okay.

This is often the main step, where the deepest change happens inside a person. Of the five steps, it's the step where people connect to their inner energy source and experience power filling them. Someone once told me he was afraid if he used this process he might "lose" his anger, maybe lose strength and shrink to indifference. Rather, it can be a moment of dramatic feelings of change from powerless agitation or fear of conflict or hopeless irritation to strong energy. That was what Ana Maria seemed to be experiencing. There's a feeling of well-being in this. It's not a sleepy calm, but a powerful, capable calm. I was mirroring her pressing her hands against her upper chest because I wanted her to be aware of her body assimilating and remembering this.

"It almost feels like ... before, part of me was wanting to say, 'well, this is just me,' but ..." She paused, shaking her head bleakly. "I've come to doubt my own beliefs." Suddenly she straightened and relaxed, as if her body had accepted her soul. "I like this. These things are important to other people too, not just me."

"You had come to doubt your own values, your own self."

"I haven't been honoring those values." She pushed her hands against her chest and said, "It's like my heart is expanding: Like, 'Gee, maybe those ideas are who I am.'"

More than in any other step, in this step I wanted Ana Maria to underline what she had just grasped. I reminded her to write it down. I wanted her to have a record of it to go back to in times of doubt. I also wanted her to have it written down in case she reconsidered her decision about James and the divorce, so she could approach him with the same clarity about it that she was feeling now herself.

For Step Four, **E: Enjoy and Embrace Your Values,** she wrote:

> *I value self-reliance and problem solving.*
> *I believe things go better in the world generally when*
> *people think for themselves and make the effort to*
> *get things right.*

These may or may not be Ana Maria's central values, but they are important ones to her. She focused on this issue first. "Self-reliance" seemed a big part of her emotional inheritance from her father—albeit along with confusion, thanks to his irritable demands. More Anger-Makeover work might highlight additional values and boost her self-confidence.

Also, her independence and problem solving were exactly the values her husband seemed to be ignoring, even belittling. Her shakiness about her values made the conflict worse, because it was harder to honor his values of harmony and cooperation for fear of having to give up her independence. It was harder to see his opposite values as complementary. She felt her identity in danger, and she had been afraid of losing herself either by staying silent, or by being demanding. Basic self-recognition as individuals with valid differences would help them both.

At least it seemed to help her. "In this relationship I've come to doubt that my self-reliance was wise."

Replacing Her Hesitancy with Confidence

"So," I said, "you don't need to minimize or question your values just because James has espoused a different set. Maybe his focus is not on independence, but on interdependence: 'We all need to reach out for help,' or 'No one is an island.'" These qualities are the opposite of independence, but they can complement it. They don't have to obliterate it.

Ana Maria and James might have been able to create a cohesive team, teaching each other an unbeatable combination like "bonded self-reliance" or "affectionate effort" or "non-dependent love." Accepting opposite and complementary values is indispensable in all relationships. Psychosynthesis, and Assagioli's work on the "Synthesis of Opposites," outline this

> *"First let these values sink in as a part of you. Then you'll be able to talk to James about them."*

basic wisdom. Yet people try to cancel out other people's ideas with their own—or, like Ana Maria, cancel out their own with the other's.

Ana Maria was starting to grasp how important it was to be herself—and maybe let James see her better as an independent thinker who works hard at holding her own. Instead of minimizing her own beliefs to become homogenized with James, she could define and keep her points of difference.

"Okay," she said. "I accept that these things seem unimportant to James. I want to be with someone who knows and honors this in me." She hadn't felt James was present, but I wasn't so sure it would be too much to ask him to honor this in her.

I wondered if starting to feel strong in herself would help her listen to his frustration, to what he was wanting. Partners are never identical; only she could decide whether she and her husband had enough interests in common to work on the shaky marriage. Part of her problem with James had been her hesitancy to accept herself.

Self-acceptance had to come first. "How rash would it be to talk to James about these values before you let them sink in as a part of you?"

"Very," she admitted.

"You may find it easier to talk to James once you finish this process and feel strong about your own beliefs and identity."

"Yes. I've felt a combative edge. My wanting to get things right has been just my little place inside, so I've been defensive. I imagine when I feel strong, his reactions won't bother me so much."

Affirming Our Values Even If We've Drifted

"One more thing," I said. "Not always having lived up to our values doesn't mean they're not our values. Someone that remembers having lied is not necessarily a hypocrite for saying, "I value honesty." Can you see that these values definitely are you?"

"Yes, I see that. I have no problem with that."

"Good," I said. She got it. I was glad.

Would this confirm her resolve to leave her husband, or would feeling less vulnerable—less as though every misstep of his was a mortal wound—let her listen better to him? They already had separated twice and attempted reconciliation. To her, this might confirm that the marriage was beyond hope, even explain why. I hoped she could at least stand up for herself without criticizing him.

And I wondered about James: Maybe he would sense the change in her and start feeling better. The marriage might already be too far gone after years of feeling hurt by each other, but what might deeply touch her would be if he started to understand her. That might not happen unless she started taking the initiative and explaining herself.

5: Understand Ways to Plug Your New Understandings into Life

In this last step, Ana Maria would test her ability to stay in touch with her newly clarified values. She now perceived her self-reliance and competence as core qualities. She needed to keep them alive and realize that they gave her expanded options. The notes she had been writing would help with her final internal task: reviewing her options. She needed to look at the solid, strong realities she had already listed in the previous four steps. They might feel like new tools. They might seem odd or clumsy at first, but she had already started to feel their power.

"Now for the last step, the final **R of POWER, Review Your Range of Options.** Here, you can brainstorm freely. We're still just reviewing possibilities, so you can feel free to consider a wide range of options, from very reserved, like not verbalizing anything, to very expressive, like having a good talk.

"Ask yourself what options you now might have with James. It doesn't mean give up your old choices. For example, you could still swallow your irritation until you finally explode at him. The good news: You could also use information from any of the previous four steps: give your picture of the problem, own the emotions you're feeling, let him know specific actions you want from him, tell your underlying values.

Ana Maria seemed to be swimming in new feelings: grief about what might have been, anxiety about the task ahead. Yet she seemed purposeful, ready to move on. "So, if you are still feeling the calm inside and a better sense of yourself," I said, giving her time to gather the helpful feelings, "it may be a whole new ball game."

Two weeks later when Ana Maria came in, she was shaking her head in amazement. "It's almost as if my new attitude was catching," she said. And she in turn seemed to be feeling cracks in the wall she had put up against this marriage. She had been able to discuss her preferences and beliefs with James with minimal hurting or criticizing. He still wished to reconcile. He felt sad but noticed things were different: He could start to understand and support her values of self-reliance and desire to do things right.

What Ana Maria Took Away with Her

As you know, not every story ends with immediate change. Ana Maria might have felt success just by beginning to rebuild her self-esteem, even if she hadn't been able to talk to James about it right away. People may not always feel the amount of immediate power that Ana Maria found, or be able to change how they act towards someone. But playing with this process will often raise spirits, sharpen thinking, and calm the mind.

Ana Maria had come in tight, self-defensive, and anxious. She had been confused about what to say to her husband, from whom she'd been separated for two weeks. She walked out still looking worn from the anguish and stress of other challenges she was going through, but she also was behaving in several fresh ways. She voiced self-assurance about an important aspect of her identity. She was clear that it was fine to be someone who believed in getting things right, as well as using her analytical abilities to figure things out before talking. There was a place for her annoyance about someone close to her "blurting out half-baked answers and depending on someone else to think for them." She also affirmed for the first time that her beliefs might be valuable for the world generally. She was beginning to embrace her values not as quirks, saying "Well that's just me," but as "useful for other people too."

The inner settling Ana Maria felt was letting her show her husband more confidence and less bitterness. He was responding with respect, which was a relief and might help heal their relationship. A more solid foundation could provide hope for the marriage.

Example 2: Converting Overboard Shame and Self-Directed Anger

Finding Anger at Your Inner Self-Punisher and Listening to It

Anger reactions can spoil not only our relationship with people close to us, but also our relationship with ourselves. I may think punitive self-judgment is just me, correcting myself. Maybe so. Shame can be curative. It wants to correct the mistake. However, punitive shame wants to punish the mistake endlessly. "Doing that was bad. You should be ashamed. Stupid." This harsh, punitive critic is not me. It's a part of me locked in a seriously harmful, resentful, punishing behavior. Yes, we must do what we can to rectify the original mistake. We also need to see and react to self-harm and punishment and put a stop to it.

The Anger Makeover can be effective for transforming self-directed anger and shame. This is something important that I didn't include in the first edition of this book. I missed it because I didn't have my present perspective, the knowledge that Self or Spirit does not punish or judge. Many people have learned at home and at school to inflict on themselves an overwhelming, deep, soul-numbing regret over mistakes, even ones made far in the past and corrected long ago. Once you notice such self-mis-treatment happening, you can use the Anger Makeover to replace the harmful self-punishing with peace and, when needed, with a quest for ways to better yourself gently and purposefully. In place of the whip, it suggests kind guidance toward self-mastery. The Anger-Makeover process looks at that urge to kick ourselves and makes positive use of it. It transforms those self-accusations.

But first we must notice if anger is present at the part of us doing self-harm and wallowing in pain. If so, it's possible we can feel our anger as a messenger, inviting transformation.

Everyone has made mistakes, some bigger than others. Fortunately, failures aren't the end of the story.

The poet Antonio Machado wrote about a dream in which

> ... I had a beehive
> here inside my heart.
> And the golden bees
> were making white combs
> and sweet honey
> from my old failures. [1]

That is the kind of transformation the Anger Makeover offers.

Once we recognize and are angry about the harm we've been doing by punishing ourselves for long-past mistakes, we can use the strong insight in that anger. It becomes the focus of an Anger Makeover. We can examine the indignation we feel when we identify with the anger. "Being in the shoes" of the anger, we're indignant about the self-punishing, about hanging on to shaming. So the anger can be a signal, alerting us to exactly what change to make.

We need that insight, because just spotting self-cruelty is hard enough in itself. We're blind to it. I link this blindness to centuries of passed-down trauma. Resmaa Menakem in his book *My Grandmother's Hands* talks about trauma. He helps people heal the trauma embedded in their bodies, both recent trauma and inherited trauma that dates back through prehistory. It's healed by facing the pain, not retaliating or sliding over it.

I feel lucky that I finally spotted my traumatic self-cruelty, and that I didn't like it. I felt angry about it. I felt angry that my shame had abandoned me in a harsh, dry place. Using the Anger Makeover, I unearthed from my anger a refreshing spring, my preference for gentleness, for letting bygones be bygones, or at least for being caring and effective in how I bettered myself. This was smart anger at my misplaced anger about my earlier misplaced anger— smart anger at the part of me that was punishing me for long ago having inappropriately unloaded anger on a friend and colleague.

The anger gave me freedom and insight. It opened me to another dimension, a higher part of me that Assagioli described in his article "Smiling Wisdom." He showed how, when we're "working with one part of [ourself]," we can keep present our "higher and real Self, a detached and smiling spectator." Ultimately, the Anger-Makeover process takes any particular anger and shows its connection to smiling wisdom.

How is it possible that punishment of all kinds can be so popular? Many people sincerely believe that revenge and punishment make sense, that they correct wrongs. They're sure that without revenge and punishment we have no morals. On the contrary, I'm clear that revenge and punishment are themselves ancient, traumatic, additional mistakes. They have been damaging to all concerned. They do much harm and questionable good. That holds true for self-revenge and self-punishment. Especially with friends and loved ones, once we feel our anger about the impulse and harshness itself, we can switch to relief and calm, and if needed, gentle correcting.

Here's my personal example. I realized I was still kicking myself about losing a relationship with a colleague and friend long ago. The self-kicking was severe: endless regret. Somehow, I managed to unmask the uselessness of that pain. Doing the Anger Makeover turned the self-damage into healing.

The self-punishment came whenever I remembered how I once blindly reprimanded a friend and colleague. I had felt that she had been wronging me with criticism. Only later did I regret how I had treated her. I came to see that I had made a mistake that often comes with deep-felt anger. I had let a combination of righteousness and resentment do the talking. I had grimly, with no smiling wisdom, laid out to her the wrong I thought she was doing. I soon discovered how self-defeating it can be to talk from impulse. For conflict with a friend to be beneficial, it can't just be impulsive talk with no caring. I'm glad that smiling wisdom has been dawning on me, albeit slowly, through the years. I now see that conflict has a chance when it includes voicing appreciation of the friendship and specifying positive behaviors preferred, and respectfully inviting discussion.

My friend didn't walk out then and there, but she abandoned the friendship. Surely, she didn't feel safe, respected, or heard. Not that the other extreme, silence in conflicts, is always better. A pause may be needed, but then also follow-up. Doing an Anger Makeover can provide self-understanding. It is a follow-up to the pause. It reveals our positive preferences and value differences. These are big improvements over knee-jerk, impulsive criticism or demands.

Now I know better. Nothing good comes from blaming or shaming our loved ones. Just to clarify, I made two big mistakes. First, I failed to do what I now urge in this book, be my loving, nonjudging, and respectful self while telling her my viewpoint, values, and preferences. Secondly, I kept on kicking myself later, going way beyond healthy remorse. Some half-conscious part of me was endlessly judging and poking at me for that now-long-past judgmental conduct toward my friend, conduct which was over and amended as much as was possible.

Anger often includes impulsive judgment, but the two aren't necessarily the same. Anger, skillfully adjusted, can cure; being judgmental and punitive mostly causes wounds. Anger wants change; judgment wants revenge. Self-anger can lead to caring self-discipline; self-judgment demands punishment, pain, even destruction.

Get Mad at the Inner Punisher

Nothing can happen until we (a) see the self-punishing, (b) grasp how wrong and harmful it is, and (c) expose it as radically different from healthy remorse. We need to get seriously concerned, separate ourselves from, even get mad at the inner punisher. We need to feel irritated about the shaming and punishing. The one that needs to change is the shamer-punisher in us. We need rightful anger, what Assagioli called "holy indignance." The shamer is a nasty, righteous part that's crippling our well-being long after the mistake has been remedied. This anger can teach us something better. We need anger directed at the punisher, the punishment, and at the vein of revenge in our society and ourselves that believes in punishment so enthusiastically.

We benefit from lovingly spending time learning from this alert, angry observer in us, learning what it wants in place of the harmful, self-punishing behavior and the resulting debilitating shame. This alert part of us can tell us what it would prefer instead from the punisher. It may be something useful and not destructive, such as caring and respect, once we've made sure the problem is over and we've done what we could. We follow the concerned anger's guidance toward the loving skill it wants the punisher to develop, such as caring, respectful appreciation of the hard-won improvements.

We find gentle, firm values for helping ourselves toward a punishment-free, joyful new life. Shame squelches joy. I'm thankful it's never too late to liberate our joy. Joy is so important. "Joy," said Assagioli, "is our duty." In my case, joy is opening my heart.

Reasons for the Confusion

My reason for creating the careful description of my conduct above is that figuring it out was a confusing task for me. One reason it was confusing is that for many years I thought my pain was simply the long-ago loss of a relationship with a friend. I came to see that there was something more: an ongoing pain that was deeply stressful to my relationship with myself. I don't think this kind of self-punishment, shame, or hatred is so unusual, but it is confusing because it takes so much work to pin down the punisher as a wrongdoer. I thought it was an inner friend. I didn't see it clearly. I needed the anger about punishing. That anger could lead to power.

So, what blocked me from seeing the additional mistake, my self-whipping? It was my grief over the original mistake of scolding a friend and losing that friendship. In addition, self-punishment is not simple. It is a mix of two opposites, punisher and punished, blame and shame. Further, while the visible, external mistake I made with my friend was easy to see, it was much harder to see the disguised, internal, sanctimonious punisher in me, let alone recognize it as harmful.

In our punishment-friendly culture, it seemed perfectly natural to let my self-punishing part keep on jabbing me. It had gone on for years. It was hidden from view or perhaps ignored because so many people think shaming and punishment are okay, effective, and necessary. The cultural norm made it almost impossible to wake up, spot the punisher, and be angry at it. I no longer see judgmentalism or punishment as part of any divine plan, but as a heavy, haunting problem.

Widespread punishment-laden religious teaching is part of our cultural norm, and I still feel after-effects from that and my own traumatic self-punishment. They dimmed my healthy, robust joy in life. I'm happily relearning that "rejoice" is not just a word. It is a delirious, excited glow. And so, I am startled seeing how society loves and approves of punishment. It keeps passing on the trauma. We inherited punishment from eons of shunning, killing, exiling, and torture—as if it were some kind of magic remedy and not our knee-jerk brain on the rampage. The lizard brain errs on the side of alarm when it errs, and that is most of the time and mostly in our relationships in daily life. So we need to wake up, in our relationships first of all, to the harmful consequences, not only to the person being punished, but also to the punisher. Punishment tries to satisfy overwhelming, deep, long-term revenge instincts. Even when we have been deeply injured, punishment compounds the injury. It doesn't fix it. As I keep emphasizing, impulse is by nature automatic and quicker than our thinking brain. We need to take this seriously and work with it, not buy into vengeance. Raw impulse disguised as "sending a message" is damaging enough in the larger society. It is especially counter-productive among family and friends and at the office. It's questionable what message acting on raw impulse sends.

The Anger Makeover and Self-Punishment

Some may question what I'm saying, since this does demand we start over at a psychological and societal level. But if you notice that you're punishing yourself, you may also notice that going through the resulting shame and regret has been debilitating and unhelpful for you. If you can get mad at the shaming-punishing committed by that vengeful, albeit very sincere part of you, you can get real benefit from the Anger Makeover. You will be discovering vital values hidden in your anger at the real culprit, your inner punisher.

If at first this anger seems like something bad, you can recall that, like all kinds of anger in this book, this anger has something valuable to teach. This angry part of you, with its alert concern, once awakened, doesn't want the draining punishment to go on. You can use the Anger-Makeover process to get guidance from the anger, guidance toward a passionate preference and deep value such as correcting gently instead of by punishing. This makes letting go of past battles possible. So does being understanding with yourself when trying to improve.

Here's a look at the five-step Anger-Makeover process as I used it to uncover important values in my anger, concern, and displeasure with my self-punishing. To recap, I had been feeling anguish and regret about a long-past mistake, and I roused myself to see the part of me that was causing the pain. It was a self-punishing part that over many years was relentlessly nagging me. When I finally felt anger at that destructive nagger, I knew this was the anger I needed to work with, the anger I could turn into caring personal power. This was the anger, distinct from anger about my original mistake, on which I focused the five **POWER** steps:

1) **P**icture the Problem
2) **O**wn Emotions
3) **W**ant Changes You Want
4) **E**njoy and Embrace Underlying Value
5) **R**eview Range of Options

Step 1, Picture the Problem.

The picture was of a half-submerged punisher berating me, lecturing me, judging me for long-past bad behavior. My anger saw the picture clearly. It was the punisher's harsh but almost subliminal message: a feeling of "How stupid. How could you scold a friend?" It was hanging in there, a portrait of revenge and self-punishing.

Step 2, Own Your Emotions, Including the Anger.

I felt anger at this thuggish punisher who was still resentful about the original mistake and kept my pain alive. I felt the leftover guilt and sadness about the hurtfulness of the old mistake. I felt compassion about my extended pain and the ongoing hurt to myself. What surprised me was the love and concern I felt for my joy-deprived self. These feelings made this a step that expanded me and took me far beyond the anger and shame.

Step 3, Want the Specific Changes You Want.

My anger would have preferred that I let go of outdated harshness, that I stop the brutal self-judging and focus on gentle ways to learn from mistakes and teach myself better behavior. This anger wanted me to drop regrets and relax, or make any needed efforts at self-correction compassionate. You don't keep your hand on a red-hot burner once you get its message. My anger preferred that I be understanding and forgive myself for mistakes, perhaps by welcoming in forgiveness from above. My anger preferred that I support myself in stopping self-blame and bring in self-love, or remove barriers to letting love flow down from above. My anger wanted me to give myself encouragement, relaxing and breathing to stop berating myself for the past and be in the present, alive and pain-free. I learned that if anything still needed fixing, I could trust that my anger would lead me to fix it with care and understanding.

Step 4, Enjoy and Embrace the Values
Underlying These Preferences.

This step offered relief by showing me an essential quality, my desire to be good and do good. This underlying quality was a value that felt deeper than the self-punishing, and it felt more effective than what I had been doing, hopelessly hitting myself over the head. It was about joy in the present after learning from painful mistakes. I believe things go better when one is compassionate in correcting oneself or anyone else. I believe that a more constructive approach than self-punishment behavior is to look directly at the self-punishment and correct it. And even when correcting it, I can be gentle and compassionate.

That means that even toward my inner punisher self, I am practicing the forgiveness that Dr. Stauffer taught long ago. I am canceling demands, turning them into firm preferences, and letting love flow toward the blamer, as in "Blamer, I'd prefer that you be in the present time, happy and gentle. I drop the demand for this. It was like a condition without which I wouldn't love you.

Instead, I let my love flow to you just the way you are." Even in correcting the blamer, I cancel any demand that it stop punishing and blaming me. I replace the demand with a firm preference. I let loving warmth flow again to my punisher self, even as it learns to relax and feel relief. Forgiveness is loving and gentle.

In the early stages I felt remorse. That was a sincere and rightful feeling, and it helped me wake up and change. But now clinging to self-judgment is hurtful, even if it seems sincere and helpful. Let me add, even though my punisher self may still have harsh habits to let go of, I can be firm about my preference for kindness and I can support its good intentions lovingly. Step 4 brought me back home to steadfast compassion, back home to my helpful, nonjudgmental self. I'm glad to lose the self-blame—and blame in general.

Step 5, Review Your Range of Options.

Step 5 doesn't let me off the hook; it opens me to an array of options. As I looked through the previous four steps for options, I made a list.

Option: Relax. Once past mistakes have been corrected, detach from outdated, persistent punishment.

Option: Think about what it means to be self-compassionate. Even if self-correction is still needed, it must be compassionate.

Option: Whenever I think of mistakes or misdeeds, whether mine or anyone else's, I could pause, notice where my body is unsettled, nurture it, and bring in my spiritual Self, which is unconditionally loving, nonjudgmental. That means being gently present to the part of me making the mistake of shaming or self-judging.

To get from my state of confusion to being my gentle spirit Self, I could use the powerful process I learned from Barbara Veale Smith, a Psychosynthesis coach, of calling to mind the profound notion of space. The awareness of space wakes me up to the reality of a nonjudgmental awareness already present and always present.

I learned from Barbara that in order to sense the reality of what I call Spirit, or the larger awareness we're a part of, it helps to be conscious of space. I can think of space and notice that space is all around and within me, continuously. Then I notice how space is like something even more vast, a nonjudgmental awareness that is already and always present. I move into an aware presence that doesn't judge me for mistakes.

This teaching has been more life-changing for me than anything I've learned since I first encountered Assagioli's Psychosynthesis, and Stauffer's Unconditional Love and Forgiveness. It gave me a keener understanding of their teachings. I not only felt myself in the presence of an immense awareness, I knew I was part of it. That knowing shifts me subtly but unmistakably to another level, a many-layered and all-encompassing level with no judgment. The word *nonjudgmental* cleared up a lot of life's puzzles, including how not to condemn myself or anyone, no matter how serious their mistakes. I saw how we're all in this together, all doing our best with our life experience .

Uniting with the nonjudging spiritual self is exhilarating. That is who we are—we're just not always conscious of it. Citing Dr. Les Fehmi's "open focus" work at Princeton, Barbara said at Undefended Heart[2] that simply being aware of space resets neural connections, predisposing us to less stress and greater ease. What a blessing that we can help ourselves to sense this larger awareness by simply being aware of physical space—any space, such as the space within atoms or galaxies or a room. At any challenging moment, the act of noticing space can open us to this larger, ineffable spaciousness. It tunes us to a contentless awareness that is nonjudgmental and noninterfering.

It beats kicking yourself. It's consciousness of consciousness. It's transformational. I needed to study this, and I found it helpful to view a video of a presentation Barbara made in Sicily. We all have this ability to expand into Self. It can help us open our heart to an angry or anxious part of us that may need a little help. Barbara published a clear and life-changing article about this in the June 2019 issue of *Psychosynthesis Quarterly*.

A friend of mine said, "Respecting someone's moral integrity sounds so good, but it does not always seem congruent with what I observe or feel from others." Others may not get it. Not judging anyone, even ourselves, is a hard concept to grasp. Yes, we still must do our part to clear the global jumble by listening with care and speaking our truth. We must improve how things work out for people, many of whom are vulnerable. On a political or international level, I understand the vitriol of our times, the temptation to assassinate, at least verbally, leaders whose moral integrity is not evident. So we start with a focus on the challenges we face simply being individuals in precious relationships. Here, if we can manage to do our part without judging anyone, our personal power is broader and freer—and much more effective.

What helps me is to remember the vast concept of space that I discussed above. Because it reminds me of a nonjudgmental awareness that is already and always present, it puts me in a broad view of reality that makes it possible to believe in a moral integrity, at the deepest levels, in everyone. It helps me feel whole. And it's much easier to lovingly engage with friends, relatives, or clients who are espousing dangerous political shifts that I oppose, or the conspiracy theories I consider not only nutsy-cuckoo but gravely harmful.

This doesn't mean going into a la-de-da position of allowing ourselves or our partners to abuse us, or to be indifferent to prejudice or crime or deliberate hurt, or even unintentional hurt. We must respond properly. Another analogy that helps me is the way good teachers deal with an out-of-control child in danger of hurting self or others. Good teachers neither judge nor punish. They do take actions, such as maintaining a safe environment, avoiding harshness that provokes outbursts, and restraining inappropriate or dangerous behavior quickly and with care. That takes planning, love, adequate staff, strength, patient eloquence, willingness to have discussions about values, and more. It's a good model for responding to abuse from our friends or colleagues, or from ourselves, as well as other mistakes.

Option: Choose to pause and understand that my mistakes (and those of loved ones) are honest mistakes. Recognize good intentions. It may feel like a big stretch, but the people in our lives are acting from their best sense of moral integrity.

Option: I can choose to become gentler by noticing and softening the hard seriousness that floods into me at certain times. This also is fairly new for me. I must tell about a recent insight. It came while I was writing this very discussion about regrets—about being alert to my own habit of serious unkindness to myself. It hit me that again and again during my lifetime, a heavy seriousness has repeatedly flooded into me. I saw that it came from absorbing, over a period from infancy well into adulthood, a disturbed belief from loving parents, guardians, teachers, and religious leaders. They passed along centuries of warnings about a loving God's eternal fires of punishment. Dogmatic, extreme, and brutal, at any age. Certain that they must protect me, they were in reality passing on severe anxiety and trauma, to me and others. Does morality fall apart when you take away hell? No, it becomes whole.

So I'm saying that I can avoid laying heaviness on myself and others by observing that after that trauma I still easily become overly serious when discussing a heavy topic. Grave warnings—still very much in vogue in our world—were an ordeal. I see the damage they did to my sweetness of spirit. Over and over, I have unhooked from this well-meant but brutal teaching. When discussing heavy topics, I still choose to be on the alert. I become conscious of my overly serious tone and invite it to soften. Even writing this, I've wondered, "Maybe I should have lightened up on this too." But that wouldn't have been honest. I consider it, clearly, a very serious issue. Meanwhile, I'll stand back, feel the anguish, be with the emotions, and let the healing go on.

I think others have felt the seriousness that crept into me. It must have seemed at times almost threatening, as if I was laying anger or blame on them. This must have added even more heaviness to that mistake long ago of laying blame on my friend and colleague. I now know that every single time I feel angry, I can remember my own trauma, soften my attitude, stay alert, and lighten up the ominous seriousness. I pray that with conscious care I will never again unintentionally cast that centuries-old, steely harshness on anyone, least of all on innocent people I care about.

Option: Choose to forgive myself. I could hold firm preferences for any changes needed, and at the same time let my love and God's flow to myself every moment. Stauffer provided a key for this. If forgiveness was needed but felt impossible, she encouraged us to let love flow down from above, into us or through us to a person we wanted to forgive. Suddenly the forgiving that had been hard for the small self felt easy. We were yielding to a divine, more-powerful love.

Option: Choose to apologize to myself for self-blaming, and replace the blame with gentleness and compassion.

Option: Choose to be a loving ally and guide to the judgmental part of me. That doesn't mean support its judging, but to appreciate its good intentions and offer a gentle space for it to soften. I'm grateful to it for sincerely trying to keep me good all through a youth that was defenseless and hemmed in with harsh teachings. I choose to tenderly soothe and heal those wounds from the stress accumulated over so many years because of the dire warnings set in stone by pious and utterly sincere caregivers. I could be gentle toward this harsh part of me and reassure it that I understand. "Punisher, I know. You believed in those unthinkably terrorizing images." A child has no defense when facing a consistent if bizarre threat of divine judgment and vengeance. I can understand how even into adulthood it adopted the judging and punishing.

Summary on Regret and Shame.

It was so confusing to me and hard for me to grasp all this, that it seems important to review what I've sorted out. Endless embarrassment, shame, and feelings of disgrace are well-known to many of us. It's so easy to say "You should be ashamed." It's not something easy to hear, and shouldn't be. It's wrong at both ends—especially because some of us are so ready either to totally block shame, or to believe it. If we believe statements like "You should be punished," there may be a shamer part inside us threatening a shamed part, ready with punishment and judgment. Self-punishment is a bad mix of two parts of us, trained punisher and longsuffering "punishee."

When we remember long-past mistakes and wrong deeds and feel painful knee-jerk self-punishment reactions, at first we may need to wake up to a mistake and correct it. But if we have done what we can to make amends, it's time to post a lookout for the brute self-punishment. Once we've fixed something fixable, it may be time to go forward. Pain extended beyond good learning and action is not healthy. It doesn't help. It harms.

The good news is that we can change these painful punisher impulses. When we notice the damage an inner punisher is doing, it's time to feel our anger about the damage. This anger knows punishing is not right. It invites us to change. To correct the punisher, we can make sure not to use more of the same naked, harsh, knee-jerk reactions. The Anger Makeover helps unleash the preferences and values within the anger. Certainly the anger wants the punisher to stop the harsh blaming. If there's correcting still needed, our anger wants the correcting done with gentle goodness and loving concern. More good news: Such a change may reconnect us to our inborn joy. That joyful being is who we deeply are and always have been.

Using the Anger Makeover, we work with our anger about the self-blame to softly transform the self-blame. We forgive the self-punishing as a mistake, yet hold a firm preference that it switch to peacefulness or gentle correcting. We stay on the lookout for painful mental replays of self-blame and make room for healing. With gentleness and caring for our past trauma, we invite peaceful internal videos in which, if better behavior is still needed, we coach, not lash, ourselves toward it.

There's plenty to do that's positive, as we follow the anger's protective preferences for gentleness, concern, and love. In those values are joy and visions of healing. We move in the direction of our firm, gentle, capable selves.

PART II

Using the Process

USING THE PROCESS

The next five sections give tips for each step along the way. But before you go on, here are a few global guidelines for the Anger Makeover.

To Get More from The Anger-Makeover Process as a Whole:

1. *Write* your answers when you can, especially at first. Later, you may be using the process unconsciously and constantly, so you won't be able to write everything, or have the need.

2. *Refer back to the guidelines specific to each step* with each new issue you go through. You'll sharpen each step as you get more practice.

3. *Take notes.* Capture the subtle surprises and the new things you learn along the way. Your notes speak to you immediately and mean a lot later.

4. *Finish.* Whenever you can, use all five steps, although it may be fine to stop part way through and use what you've learned.

5. *Keep using the process.* I've made mistakes in conflicts when I didn't use the process and had my most successful interactions when I did. And using it to review memories of past mistakes has flipped those mistakes into success, great calm, and confidence, because I was learning about who I was.

Feel free to use these guidelines imaginatively, whether you take five minutes on a given struggle or five weeks. Grab a copy of the worksheet on pages 56 and 57 and use it flexibly, however you like. You may want to scribble furiously for ten minutes on each step—especially if the issue is emotionally charged for you. Or you may spend thirty minutes writing about Step One, then four minutes going through the other four. Trust the process.

You can zip through the notes in the next chapters quickly, or take your time. It all depends on which steps you are most ready to learn from. I encourage you to experiment with the Anger Makeover regularly. As you do so, in your own way, of course, the process opens you to your personal rainbow of capabilities. You'll get back every minute you put in, and more: new vitality and surprise benefits in your relationships and interactions. Great new things happen each time you use these steps. I hope these guidelines help you get the most you can each time.

STEP 1:

PICTURE THE PROBLEM

Lose Expletives, Get Specific

This first step is the only one that doesn't focus on you. It focuses on the other person to get clear about exactly what your friend or loved one said or did. That gets you away from your judging, name-calling, or put-downs. Instead of wasting energy in those ways, you start right out untwisting any mistakes. You need the right picture as you go on to look for your true power. In the rest of the steps, you focus inside you and reshape your anger energy so you can put it to better use. You get to feel the power in your own emotions, preferences, values, so you can make better choices.

When I led a workshop on the Anger Makeover in Chicago, a participant who headed a counseling program there said, "I was afraid you were going to teach us to avoid anger and find sweetness and light. Instead, the focus right from the start was on our anger about an issue." His comment was exactly right. Step One of the Anger Makeover is the opposite of turning away from bad feelings to get to sweetness and light. We use skillful tools to light up the problem itself and our reaction to it. That's where energy and wisdom are waiting for us: in a good picture of the problem and what we learn from our reaction to it.

In fact, anger can erupt and catch us off guard. What to do first? The 13th century poet Jalaluddin Rumi, in his very popular poem "The Guest House"[3] tells us new feelings are like surprise guests.

And what is his surprise advice? "Welcome and entertain them all!" His lists of surprise guests include "meanness" and "malice." The Anger Makeover helps us use that advice. It gives us effective steps to take as soon as we have welcomed any angry reaction. To reap the great energy in a newly arrived reaction, we pause and shift gears. And we learn why Rumi says each new momentary awareness "has been sent as a guide from beyond." We discover preferences and values in our anger. We are guided to solid ground.

The Section on the Anger Makeover in Relationships explored ways to use the process. And maybe you've already written responses on worksheets (**P-O-W-E-R** Worksheet—see pages 56 and 57) or maybe you took mental notes. Those notes are a fine start too. Not all the tips I give here necessarily apply to each incident you decide to review, so just use what works each time.

If you haven't already selected a personal incident or issue to process, I encourage you to pick one now. Maybe that employee showed up late again, or your teen partied instead of doing homework, or a motorist called you a jackass (or cut you off and you called him a jackass).

It helps to write down two things in the first ("**P**") position on the worksheet: the person's exact conduct, and real or possible harm done. Below are notes on each of those.

1) Note What the Person Said, Did, or Omitted.

In describing the observable behavior that irritated you, you can start with the general description and narrow down to the concrete actions or words. You want a workable word picture. A short sentence should do it. As you go along, pay attention to what's happening in your body, where you feel it, and what you feel.

When you're angry about something the other person failed to do, it may seem impossible to name anything concrete or observable. The Anger-Makeover process can help here, since you can make just as vivid a picture of what someone omitted as what they committed. For example, suppose you started with a sentence like "She wouldn't give me a straight answer." That's not specific, so you can simply name the concrete behavior she is avoiding, such as "She didn't say she was doing 65 mph." There's your picture of the problem.

So now, before we move on to the second part, the harm done, you may find it helpful to jot down notes to a few questions.

Have I Written a Concrete Behavior?

This means observable words or actions. It's like asking, have I written down something I could see and hear in a video? If you wrote, "My sister is so thoughtless," that's not concrete. Instead, the video would have shown the phone waking you up at seven on a Sunday and you hearing your sister's cheery voice saying, "Did I wake you?" That's the concrete picture. You could write, "My sister called me again at seven on Sunday and said, 'Oh, did I wake you?'"

Did I Accurately State My Case, or Did I Overstate It?

Look for exaggerations: always, never, every time, constantly, forever. You get a star for every absolute you weed out—here and in your later thinking or dialog.

A man wrote about his wife, "She *never* gives me credit for trying. She *always* picks at my driving." (I put the absolutes in italics.) His more modest rewrite was specific and concrete—and a bit amusing. "As we drove over the bridge, I didn't change lanes or pass, because she hates it when I do. So then she turned on me and said, 'Why are you driving so slow?'"

A woman wrote, "Every time I try to say how I feel, he interrupts." Here's her rewrite: "Three times I started to say how I felt, and he interrupted me each time."

Do you feel the difference? The revisions may take more words, but they are simpler—and more real and sometimes more fun. Personally, I start to feel calmer just thinking in specifics instead of absolutes. And when I talk in specifics to my wife, family, or friends, I feel on more-solid ground. I get a more positive response from them, too. Using specifics can clarify things in your own head and make a discussion go more smoothly.

Here's a serious disadvantage to me of overstating my case. When the painting in my head shows the other person as the big bad wolf, it discourages me from speaking up, and the situation feels harder to change if I do speak up. These absolutist words can turn the images in my own head from molehills into mountains.

In situations where we are more inclined to use our silent mode, it sometimes helps to notice that the problem is worth talking about. That counteracts our impulse to retreat into thinking "Oh, it's not worth the trouble." Making problems more specific and finite makes them more workable, so we are more ready to bring them up and talk about them when appropriate. And then we can see how to talk about possibilities and preferences instead of framing everything as impossible and a reason to be silent and distant.

In situations where we tend to spout off too quickly, we tend not to pause. By not pausing, we may put up a word wall between us and our partner or family member. Doing an Anger Makeover helps us pause, and use the pause. We can settle down, honor ourselves and our deeper knowing, and realize how much stronger our positive preferences and values are than spouting off. A quick use of the Anger Makeover points us in a better direction.

There may be times when we have already spouted off and think it's too late for an Anger Makeover. But no, we can still use one to get clear about what we want. We may still be able to sidestep an urge to make a demand or declare an ultimatum. We have elbow room to explore what's possible. And perhaps we can chart a better course forward in the relationship.

Have I Stopped My Assumptions About the Person's Attitude or Intent?

Examples of this would be "He hung up on me because *he's jealous,*" or "She's suing me *to get revenge*" Even when these guesses about the other person's bad attitude are right, drop them. Wake up to lots of other possibilities. Name the behavior. The truth may be that she's deeply hurt and scared, not vengeful. Dropping the revenge assumption may let you see the hurt and fear and give you a clear picture. Imagery can help here. You can calm yourself, sit down, and ask for an image to come to you in answer to a question such as "What might make my assumption not true?" or "What might another possibility be?

Have I Described What the Person Did Rather Than Judge Who She or He is?

When you attribute unchangeable states to any person, take note. Be willing to question your belief that your loved one can never change, as well as willing to restate the problem as something changeable. I try to flag guesses or judgments that I have about the person, such as "He's just not too bright," "She's impossible," or "What a jerk!" Notice how portraying someone's actions or words, even mistakes, as permanent traits locks down your thinking. If conflicts tend to bring out your nice side—using your reserved skills more than your expressive ones—you may be prone to placing too many limitations on yourself. You may need more freedom to express yourself and stand up for your values. If you guess that your spouse will never be able to be polite around the house, your guess is working against preferences you could be framing and expressing. By noticing the specifics you want to see changed, you get your process going in a promising direction.

We often think others are the barriers, whereas what's stopping the process might be our own thinking. If I think, "This company is never going to change," I do several unproductive things: 1) I limit my ability and willingness to change my habit of silence, 2) I don't even try to make improvements, and 3) I keep myself from noticing the people or events that could help make changes. I need freedom to continue always exploring my vision of what I want, along with my imagery about what I could be getting from my family, my boss, my company, my government, or the world. Then, after a while you may have that serious discussion and a chance to shed your light on the subject.

Have I Described the Picture I See in Front of Me Now, Rather Than Projecting My Inner Pictures and Distortions Based on Memory?

The present picture has impact by itself. Deal with the present. It doesn't help to confuse things by adding your inner guesses and judgments. You may remember the example in the first Section, when June's supervisor Marcie suddenly withheld June's promotion. June thought, "She's either jealous or afraid of me." That was a distortion coming from inside June. The picture currently in front of her was simply, "Marcie withheld my promotion. She even told me the bad news on the very day she herself had led me to expect a promotion." That was already a stark picture. It was important that June hear the reasons why the promotion was withheld, rather than invent her own reasons. This reduces the chances June would leave feeling hurt, angry, or discouraged, based on what she imagined.

2) Have I Neglected the Potential Harm Done by the Person's Words or Action?

Have you ever noticed that when we are in our gentler mode, we tend to minimize the real pain we may have felt? We might deny feeling hurt or angry even if a friend went behind our back instead of talking to us directly, or when a spouse or buddy has ignored an achievement we're proud of, for fear of losing ground in some ongoing relationship battle. And have you noticed how our reserved side hates to rock the boat? We may say "Oh, it's no big deal," even if something is important to us. We may hate even seeing how a friend or spouse offended us.

Citing potential harm doesn't necessarily mean we immediately blow the whistle or say, "Hey, Earl, you screwed things up." It's more about opening our own eyes—being alert to reality ourselves and not minimizing our hurt.

With that in mind, we look at what the person said or did, and describe for ourselves any adverse effects it may have had. Honestly list any losses and damages you have evidence of: damage to yourself, to the person, to relationships, to others, to the world today, to the world in the future, and so on. Here are questions you can ask yourself, to help you complete your picture of the problem.

Have I Minimized or Exaggerated the Harmful Effects of the Person's Action?

For example, has it harmed anyone's emotional vitality or spiritual focus or given the wrongdoer undue influence?

Am I Noticing the Self-inflicted Hurt to the Offending Person?

What are the disadvantages or pain it brings to the one acting and speaking wrongly?

Do I Recognize the Harmful Ripple Effects of the Person's Behavior?

Were the loved ones of the primary parties hurt? How about their loved ones, colleagues, clients, or customers?

Have I let Myself Recognize Potential Damage to Relationships?

Not only how do people get hurt, but how do the ties that bind them get hurt? Ties of trust, love, affection, comfort, camaraderie, and cooperation can suffer. What someone says or does can sometimes damage or destroy delicate cords binding larger communities.

STEP 2:

OWN YOUR OWN FEELINGS, IN YOUR BODY AND EMOTIONS

The Mix of Feelings That Ride In With Your Anger

This step momentarily takes the focus off the external threat, real or imagined, and opens you to the inner burst of emotions, which may at first seem like anger only. Opening to the emotions that come with the anger is momentous. These other emotions often get overlooked, yet the concern or fear or love may be more important and central than the anger. Or your shock, loss, dread, love, hate, or sadness. Again, as in Step One, as you go along, pay attention to what's happening in your body, what you feel, and where you feel it.

If you are alert enough not to let the anger take over the whole stage, you have more freedom to be your full self. It's helpful not to let anger hog the spotlight, especially with loved ones. What makes anger stand out is the huge flash it makes, and that flash is usually way out of proportion to the external event causing it. The event is minor; the anger is existential. Could it be that in our psyche all anger has some link to the fear of extinction—and not just your extinction as an individual, but that of your tribe, race, and future descendants? Noticing your mix of feelings helps get you back to reality.

This may make it easier to grasp what a blow an oversized knee-jerk is. Imagine someone else is getting sharp or mean with you over a small mistake of yours. Yes, it's painful. When we realize our scolding or complaining or angry tone is causing pain, it's clearer that we all need to make sure our anger stays in bounds, especially with small issues.

It may be hard to recall times you yourself felt like blowing a friend or loved one out of the water. When humans are in a cool state, they can't adequately recall a hot state, one of those moments of needing to escape a threat or get rid of an interruption, or wanting to yell. If you can imagine a hot state, maybe you can also imagine the change you would experience if you could replace that feeling of "What the hell!" with an "I" statement such as "I'm feeling very startled and angry." The trigger reaction was probably focused outward, on the threat ("You're a menace!"). When you're stating a feeling, you're focusing more inward ("I'm alarmed!"). That inward focus changes things—and you're not weaker, but stronger. You're not feeling so vulnerable, dangerous, hotheaded, and destructive. You've moved your focus from the external "threat" to your inner emotional experience and physical sensations. It's not always easy to do, but it's the beginning of lifelong liberation.

And even then, sometimes it's also helpful to back off a bit from "I'm angry!" Saying it that way may be too harsh for many friends and colleagues. Additionally, those words may tie you too close to the raw feeling, so it feels overwhelming—more like "I am anger!" You can change your experience by using the statement "I feel angry" or "I have this feeling of anger." You're less identified with the anger, less "being" the anger. You move to being your self, that is, being identified with the "I," yourself, the solid person who has the anger. We can learn to go from being shaky and hotheaded to simply allowing and accepting strong emotion. Every time we grasp that who we *are* is something substantial, something more than the feeling, we change a little. By making the shift to being who we are, we lower our chance of staying stuck in feeling as if we are our reaction. That is not who we are. We are always a being that is far more than a reaction, no matter how convincing a reaction feels at the time.

Hanging on to the reaction, I lose touch with self. It's better not to prolong that. Each time I stay lost in shock or anger over some seeming affront, I run more risk of staying stuck believing in my snap judgment. If I stay convinced that the friend or colleague can't quite be trusted to be sane or have good intentions, that's leftover hormones, usually far from the whole, rich truth.

My colleague Jan expressed how fear is a part of all this. I agree with his assessment strongly enough to give you his words.

> Your timid person in that previous Section was a fearful person, so moving from fear and moving from anger are the same process, just beginning at two different points. Fear, I think, is the earliest point for most of us. Anger can develop when we don't acknowledge the fear. Sometimes when I see the fear and get into it and work with it, the anger evaporates. I am using the book now to inspire my attempts to help someone to move from fear to power. So, the process might also be called "the fear (or shock, or loss) makeover."

Some of us are more hesitant, wisely skeptical of urgent impulses we feel coming from our expressive side. Still, we may be too paralyzed by fears and old habits of silence to be our best selves. And others of us are quicker in conflicts, wisely skeptical of being too reserved. We too may be hijacked by our extreme discomfort. We may jump in and not be our best selves. With care and attention, we can learn from each other how to combine our best expressive and reserved skills.

I used to say that folks who use their reserved skills more

than their expressive could learn a thing or two from folks handier with their expressive skills. But let's be sure not to imitate someone whose expressive skills have been replaced by impulsive reactions and aggressive weapons. The best expressive skills are loving expressions of preferences and values. As we develop our expressive skills, it's important not to pick up bad habits that we see modeled by someone whose expressiveness has gone overboard into aggression or hostility. Our brains are complex, and at those hot times the brain may pick right up on an aggressive person's reactive nastiness or inflexibility. And so we too may end up catapulting from reserved, not to expressive, but all the way to abusive.

Better to learn to alternate reserved tools and expressive tools. Avoiding abuse may be hard because our knee-jerk impulses instantaneously block the forebrain's thoughtfulness, and we may end up believing the judgments imprinted instantly by an impulse. The Anger Makeover can help us gain awareness not just of our impulses but also of the sudden dislikes sticking to us after we think we're free of the impulses. Survival instincts shake us because they were built to assume the worst for safety's sake, but it's a mistake to hold on endlessly to those worst-case suspicions. It would be sad if we didn't examine a dislike that arrived with an impulse, and so we ended up stuck with lingering feelings of dislike, even for someone with whom we live or work. It's sad if a coworker or someone you're close to is forever assuming something bad about you. It's also sad if you are assuming something bad about someone close to you. As you may have noticed in your life, assumptions implanted by our primitive brain can create walls.

What about people who are more comfortable with their outspoken or emotionally expressive side when conflicts arise? How can they use better communication tools? Yes, they and anyone may be more aware of their emotions, but they also at times, when a colleague or partner criticizes them, may want to argue. So they may be unaware of the emotion, experiencing only the urge to argue. Fighting beats what they really need to do: pause, think, and question the urge. Before they know it, they may let fly and spoil the opportunity for conflict intimacy.

A more-expressive friend wanted me to pass along the following:

> A trigger-happy expressive person may also not be aware that mindlessly letting fly with our negative emotions may seem like an expression of personal power, but it's the opposite. Being out of control may feel good to the one who is venting, and it may intimidate someone who is more hesitant—but real power, the kind that creates lasting results, can only be exercised consciously.

Another expressive person stated emphatically that she does not feel good when venting:

> As a venting expressive—and I'm not proud of that at all—venting is simply a coping mechanism and sadly a very temporary relief. Maybe other expressive people feel good when venting, but I sure don't. To me the feeling is very intense. In the moment, it is an extreme need to relieve pressure in order to prevent an explosion.

She deserves credit for not letting her venting get explosive. And I would encourage her to use the Anger Makeover as soon as she can. Once she gets the hang of it, she can even use it in the moment. She may feel the deep relief and healing, especially from Step 4, Enjoy Your Values. Her precious values may be getting buried by brain reflexes. Having a friend or a professional counselor guide her in using the Anger-Makeover process may give her tremendous relief, because the reaction can be so intense. It's often hard to respond from that inner, more centered energy that we spoke of in the Section on power.

Some of us are just more hesitant as a matter of course. And it may be wise to be aware and skeptical of our expressive side's impulses. We also may know it would be wise to speak up, but we are just too paralyzed by fears to be our best selves. And some of us are often more expressive. We may be wisely aware of our reserved side, but just be too hijacked by our extreme discomfort to be our best selves.

And some people are very emotionally aware. They'll give you a list of their feelings at the drop of a hat. At times you may think they talk a little too much—but here are three topics where we can learn from them about owning emotions: 1) "letting off steam" but in private and within limits, 2) naming our emotions, and 3) noticing our mix of emotions. As we examine each of these, here is another useful perspective from a more-expressive friend.

These three considerations are also very good to help the emotionally impulsive person to learn to step back and privately practice self-restraint. They will have some will available for restraint when the impulse to blurt something arises in a relationship. These suggestions are a way for the trigger-happy person to learn to become conscious of the feelings that usually get expressed before the person is even aware of what is there.

Let Off Steam? Or Not?

This question feels very different to people on opposite ends of the expressive-reserved teeter-totter. I'll try to offer help to both.

Here's a tip, not just for us folks that hide our emotions way more of the time. One good way to get more comfortable owning feelings is to write freely, to state on paper our feelings about the disturbing thing the person said or did. Kitsi Watterson, my writing teacher and author of *Not by the Sword,* said that sometimes when she is trying to write and feels stuck or confused, she takes out a pen and pad and just scribbles furiously. As she told us this, her black hair framed a dark look on her face. "I might find myself letting off steam about a recent issue or just venting all the invective I feel at someone... even if it feels destructive," she laughed, "and is full of profanity."

"You really do that?" one of her students asked her. I saw her laughter stop abruptly. Her eyes flashed as she stared momentarily into space and nodded, "I certainly do." She seemed to be remembering a yet-unfinished storm of drumming heartbeats and rushing blood. Her furious scribbling gets her through emotional blocks to her writing. She gets feelings and thoughts off her chest and onto paper. She hurts no one. "Then I tear up the paper in little pieces," she said, "and put the pieces in two different trash cans." Since no one will be able to put them together, she knows her emotional writing is private. That gives her freedom to discover exactly what's bugging her.

If you are someone who needs encouragement to write safely and simply not keep it in a journal, this tip may validate your preference. Anyone can use that same little procedure in the Anger-Makeover process. Some people feel particularly guarded about Step One, Picture the Problem, and Step Two, Own Your Emotions. They can simply write, tear it up, and sort out a truer, more objective picture and the true emotions.

Can letting off steam about a family or work matter help us grow by owning our emotions? Maybe, when we do it in private, with limits. It may help especially if we generally live on our emotionally reserved side in conflicts. For people at ease with their more-expressive side, letting off steam—only in private—may help by letting them ride out the storm on their own until it calms and they can see their wildness objectively and not lay it on the other person. But if they end up open to their own side only, a rant may not be the place to start. If it makes it harder to welcome two-way interaction, they may still have other work to do.

For those of us who usually draw on our very nice side, letting off steam—in our own private space—may be a good thing. We need to observe limits of mental and physical safety. Writing in a journal or finding someone to talk to is a good idea any time you feel teary, can't get your mind off what happened, become physically drained, can't sleep, or feel hopelessly frustrated. This kind of letting it out or getting it off your chest may be especially useful, even necessary, for times when we usually hold in our feelings of frustration and hear ourselves saying things like "It's no big deal." We may keep things so calm and sweet on the outside that we're not fully aware that we feel like raging.

You hit your thumb with a hammer and let out a blue streak. Usually you just annoy or offend those who hear you. Perhaps someone at work routinely rages at "those fools running the company." It may not feel as though there is any harm, but the person may end up out of the company. If a person is already aroused physically (pulse racing, fists clenched) ranting and raving in public or in private will not increase insight. It will increase the pulse and adrenaline even more. When we are already in touch with our anger, that's a good time not to let off steam. There's no need. Walk, or talk it out with a good friend in private. "But if you're at work," said a very expressive person, "expressives like me have to be careful to not talk it out too much." She had learned that at work we may need to take extra care to guard our privacy.

Two Guidelines for Limits to Letting Off Steam:

Yes, letting go of emotions in a raving tirade may be helpful—but not without clear limits: 1) don't assume bad intent, and 2) keep all rants to yourself.

1) Don't assume Bad Intent.

First, not assuming you know someone else's intentions. Write whatever comes out; just don't buy in to the verbal abuse or accusations. The Anger Makeover helped June to see and curb her own mind-reading when she was at the computer company mentioned in Section One. As you may recall, her supervisor Marcie and Marcie's supervisor Barry had abruptly decided not to give June a promotion, even after they had said it was probably coming.

"I was furious inside," she said. "They should never have sprung this bad news on me the day I was expecting the promotion. I felt mad enough to kick things." She had instead started scribbling her feelings and thoughts in a notebook. The first thought was, "You don't care about employees." Yet in fact, Marcie had a lot of respect for June. She knew June, younger than she, had already helped create a good software program.

June commented later, "It was good to get on paper how sure I thought I was about Marcie's intentions." She had wondered on paper whether Marcie felt threatened. Maybe Marcie unconsciously wanted to damage June's place at the company. "On paper I could explore that and discard it instead of saying it. If anything, Marcie is too caring and conscientious."

Yes, Marcie had made a mistake in not letting June know sooner that the promotion was not coming yet, and not telling June what she needed to do to get one; but it was an honest mistake. "Marcie's not trying to put me in my place. If I had believed my own mind-reading about her intentions it would only have soured me—and my relationship with her. It's a good, friendly, working relationship with lots of mutual respect."

2) Keep All Rants to Yourself.

Here's that second guideline when letting off steam: Whether you're writing or using some physical method like beating a pillow, any ranting is for your ears only, to let *you* get a handle on your feelings and thoughts, not to slap half-baked judgments on the other person.

One of my divorce-recovery seminar participants in New Mexico said he got big relief by yelling his anger and pain into the canyon, literally. No human would hear, just the jackrabbits and armadillos. That's a clear, absolute limit. Don't let a private rant show up in your face-to-face interactions. And it might be very helpful to write a ranting letter to your offending colleague, friend, or loved one, but you must remember it is for your awakening only and know you will definitely not ever send it. Lots of people write e-mails they never send. Some unfortunately get sent accidentally. If the email is a response to someone, the key is, if you're venting, first take all names out of the to: and cc: lines. A reader who had seen enough blaming, accusations, and ranting agrees.

She insisted, "Never send or voice your rant—even if you have had the bad habit for years. Stop. It is not too late to stop. Even though you will keep screwing up and doing it again. Try again. And again. This is true at home and at work. For those who struggle with impulse control and are generally expressive, this can't be overemphasized." A very reserved friend of her dad's told her about an old Bob Newhart skit. To see it you can Google, "Bob Newhart just stop it." Start about 1:20 into the 6-minute clip.

Yes, that Newhart skit is on target. And therapeutic. And to help you stop you can do an Anger Makeover.

June, in the scenario above went through the Anger-Make-over process, and it let her consciously choose what to say to Marcie. June knew it would not be appropriate to tell her off or put her in her place with a hasty accusation. "The other reason I needed to do the Anger Makeover," June observed, "is that, because of the type of person I am, I run the risk of holding it all in. I shut down. Then I walk around absent-minded and preoccupied."

As it turned out, it was a good thing June had used the process, because later she was surprised to hear herself blurting out her feelings. Fortunately, they were her true emotions. By then, the Anger-Makeover process had given her the words she needed, in place of angry accusations.

"It happened when Marcie sat down to go over a new proce-dure with me," June said. "She asked me, 'So, how are you doing?' Her question caught me off guard. I glanced at her face. It was like she was forcing herself to keep eye contact with me.

Jane said she wondered if Marcie was so uneasy because she was hiding something. Or was she ashamed, or putting on a busi-ness-as-usual mask? Unfortunately June was again simmering with hurt and anger, because she had just looked back at Marcie's earlier note explaining why Marcie had not promoted her.

"The words, 'Oh, fine,' automatically came into my head," June said. "My own business-as-usual mask tried to express that. But my simmering inside wouldn't let me say it. For a moment, the two parts of me struggled. I tried to speak but couldn't. Now I knew I had to explain my stammering silence and blurted out, 'Oh, I guess I'm still mad as hell.'"

Aside from the mild profanity, it turned out to be a good opener. Marcie looked suddenly sad, as she softly said, "I'm glad you said how you really feel."

"After a few moments of silence," June said, "Marcie went

back to her office. I saw her typing madly at her computer for ten minutes. Then she met with me to apologize for how she had handled things. We ended up having a good talk. If I hadn't done an Anger Makeover, I'd probably just have gone on showing a mask—a nice manners mask, but a depressed and preoccupied one. Or, worse, I'd have blurted out this mean frontal attack from my earlier private scribbling stage, like 'What kind of supervisors are you? You're screw-ups. You and Barry both. And your stupid evaluation system rots.' It would have led to hurt, confusion, and lots of wasted time doing repair work on our relationship—and on my credibility as an emotionally balanced employee in a corporate system."

More Reasons to Let Off Steam, But in Private:

Keep the above limits in mind. I'll keep harping on them as we go on. Especially if you're already fully in touch with your anger, you may be able to learn to think first before you let off steam, especially when the person you're mad at (or bystanders) are present. For ranting to be effective, everyone needs precautions: safety, private space, and a purpose. An expressive colleague wanted me to underline those last sentences. She considered them most important for her. Ranting can get you angrier than you were in the first place.

To Enjoy the Thrill? No.

So is there ever a good reason to let off steam (again, in private only)? Self-indulgence is not a good reason. The thrill is not a good reason, nor is the feeling of satisfaction. A friend suggested that instead of ranting, you can give yourself a shot of dopamine from a better source by playing a quick game to get your mind off it. Looking at something funny online has also helped her. Otherwise, she said, she stews—which is where she said the Anger Makeover process helps, by providing some structure.

To Find Your World of Feelings.

Sometimes we humans have been locked into a reserved style so long that we don't know what we feel, until we vent. Maybe that's the origin of the pop psychology myth that says if you're angry you should let it out—as if it's okay anytime with anyone. If you're lucky, it may work in a specific instance, depending on who hears it. Even then, there are costs, and the costs may be wide-ranging and long-lasting.

To Avoid Ailments.

Research has long tied habitual physical and emotional stress responses to serious ailments such as heart attack and stroke. Often, a person can feel better by getting the mind off the topic or thinking of it in a new way. To feel better in the long run, it's best not to take a drink, unless it's water, or eat the chocolates. Say yes to taking a walk or going for a run. Physical activity is even better than writing, or reading a passage from a favorite inspirational book, meditating, praying, remembering things you're proud of, or doing yoga. Sometimes you can do these things to get away from it for a spell, but don't keep the adrenaline pumping by letting it out. Use the Anger-Makeover process, later or right away, to think it through and put the energy into positive purposes.

To Learn New Skills.

Back to the true purpose of letting off steam: It's not to practice being tough, because you're more likely to be harsh, not strong. The purpose of letting off steam is not to change your personality. It's to experiment with new practices. In a situation where someone already tends to show his or her outspoken side more than the reserved side, I urge even more caution about sounding off. Some people already do plenty of ranting. Aggressive, impulsive, and overtly controlling people need to give steady attention to slowing down and gaining control of their thoughts, words, and actions.

To Clear Up Your Confusion.

Yes, maybe let off steam (with precautions) if you feel agitated and your own feelings and thoughts are yet again numbed or confused. People who are typically mild-mannered have a hard time taking care of themselves, claiming their rights, and being self-confident in conflicts. For them private ranting and other practices like beating pillows may be good, especially if done with care and perhaps professional help. By getting their thoughts out where they can see them, they may learn things. To readers at ease with their reserved skills this might seem natural. To those more at ease with expressive skills it might be a surprise to hear that reserved people can learn more about themselves from a private rant. A usually more-expressive reader said this information made her realize she hadn't understood someone in a past relationship. This concept, that strong feelings could be hidden or confusing, was foreign to her. Even after talking about it, she said it still seemed strange to her, though she could accept it intellectually.

To Establish Our Rights and Others' Rights.

Still, those familiar with their reserved tools need to sustain their usual, well-practiced respect for others' rights even as they learn to acknowledge their own rights. Even if they keep neglecting their own rights and feelings, they still need to remember that this isn't one or the other. It's not about affirming our rights or others' rights. We're shooting for our rights as well as others' rights. Good two-way communication includes hearing the feelings, preferences, and values from both sides.

To Stop Racing Thoughts.

One purpose of a controlled rant could be to stop the motion of the thoughts running around in your own head. It can stop them if we're willing to write down the feelings in our rant and acknowledge each of them. Otherwise the thoughts can at least intermittently cycle over and over for days, weeks, or even years. It's beneficial to simply acknowledge our thoughts and feelings to ourselves so we can sort them out.

To Make Better Decisions.

Within the ranting is the emotion of anger, and perhaps also hurt, loss, or other emotions such as, thoroughly disgusted. We may need to name, experience, honor, and own what's there before we can decide what to make of it. We can discuss it with a counselor or friend, use the energy to stand up for ourselves, maybe sometimes let the other person in on more of what's going on inside us. We may think we can cement the emotions over, deny them and their energy, or discard them, but one of the purposes of a rant, at its best, is to start transforming the energy into something usable. Yes, we want disidentification; no, that does not mean eliminating the emotion. Once you have done an Anger Makeover to redirect the energy of an anger reaction, then it will feel like a different emotion. It feels different, because it is different. It's less anger and more personal values and power.

To Understand the Bursting Energy—and Transform and Use It.

Taking time in private to sort out feelings allows us to develop a strategy for how to collect the energy and unleash it constructively. And we can be prepared, before something triggers our anger again. We need lots of practice to get good at self-expression. A good reason to let off steam is to start the process of tapping a fire inside you that has a precise purpose, one not to be overlooked. You can learn to go into and through the wild energy and get to a precise piece of your power. You can get clearer about who you are and what's important to you. Once you get your feet on the ground it's easier to let your friend or associate know how you feel about something—and let your community benefit from your good ideas.

Letting off steam in private is especially powerful if you can keep remembering your underlying confidence and respect for the person you're thinking of. But when you're feeling hurt and angry, confidence, love, and respect don't come easily. They're easier once you've done an Anger Makeover and gotten back to your values and your Self. Otherwise, it may feel hopeless to try to express emotions with power. It's useful to think at more-expressive, less-reserved times that emoting without awareness may feel terrific, but you may be wasting the energy—or worse, creating hurt and havoc.

Naming Our Emotions

Don't be too sure you already know what is going on inside you, because the questions in the Anger Makeover may unearth a different issue, or uncover additional or deeper ones. To discover what's there, it helps to name or describe as many emotions and sensations as you can detect. If you do this before you go back to talk to the person who sparked your frustration, you run less risk of feelings gushing out before you discover them. When that happens it's a surprise, even to you. Or worse, you manage to keep your customary lid on your emotions and end up not feeling much of anything. Sometimes typically meek people get out of touch with their physical and emotional feelings, and before they are aware of anger, it escalates to rage. They're busy telling themselves, "It's no big deal," or "It'll pass." So they go ahead and do what they've learned. They keep their objections to themselves and run the risk of entering the numb world of the depressed. Additionally, they may develop ulcers. If we don't act—that is, find a way such as the Anger-Makeover process to transform important energies—our body often takes the hits that we're protecting our friends or partners from feeling. This book can eliminate hits to self or others.

Because we who are typically "meek folks" misinterpret "the meek shall inherit the earth," we may think we're superior and assume everyone else should respect us. However, if we're not careful, by not respectfully *sharing* our view, we shall also inherit resentment, depression, numbness in our bodies and feelings—

and unexpected blowups. And as the non-meek know, that's absolutely true for them as well when their sharing lacks respect. Better we should notice our feelings earlier on, name them, and keep our pot from boiling over. Part of the Anger-Makeover work is like surveillance of the hiding places of our feelings and thoughts. We need to take note of what's going on in our emotional world. Another part is exploration of what those feelings mean to us. Once we take focus from our partners' and coworkers' mistakes and focus on ourselves, to know what we're feeling and thinking, we may have a better chance of talking about our feelings, thoughts, wants, beliefs, and deep values before they turn to rage.

Containing Emotions by Renaming Them

You can change your emotions. Our mix of emotions at times is vast, and so we can often switch our attention. Of course, we do it all the time. I heard a friend say, "Well, I'm not going to sit here and mope. Who can I call and have fun with?" And it works: She focuses on having fun or doing something different that grabs her imagination. Important values and beliefs come back into focus for her, and that changes how she feels.

Please don't take this as encouragement to repress or deny an emotion by forgetting it. A gifted friend of mine said he developed a practice with his wife to temporarily set an emotion aside, so that his subpersonality that felt it strongly wouldn't get stuffed or abandoned or ignored. It may be important to practice making agreements with yourself to come back to an emotion when you are better able to deal with it constructively, or when circumstances are more favorable. Yes, that may take a lot of practice and discipline. It's almost a process in itself like the Anger Makeover or cognitive-behavioral therapy or mindfulness, so give yourself time to play with it.

Or you can even make a decision to transform the energy of this emotion into something slightly different. I find this doable. I taught a client we'll call Greg to use this old trick from Dr. Albert

Ellis, author of many books on how our thinking affects our emotional states. Ellis regularly taught this concept throughout his long career: subtly renaming a feeling. For example, he suggested switching from "I'm outraged" (which feels out of control) to "I'm extremely annoyed" (which is still strong but is in your control). Get the difference? Just calling it outrage can make it feel infinite and scary; annoyance is more contained. You can choose what you want your mind to focus on, and so your emotions change.

There's more good news about this technique of Ellis's. We can change the type of feeling we're having about an issue. By changing from helpless rage about, say, how your neighbors let their dog bark in the middle of the night, to powerful annoyance or irritation about it, you feel a difference. And pause for a moment and notice the following. It's important. Give it time to marinate if necessary: Again, this is different from trying to tone down the feelings. You're switching to something that's also intense—but something that leaves you feeling intact and strong instead of out of control and desperate. Instead of staying stuck or intolerant, you can do something about the issue. This is exactly what you may often experience when you use the Anger-Makeover process and switch from a trigger reaction to a strong, deep value. You're on track to speak and act constructively.

There's a time for everything, from slogging in the swamp or dark forest to striding along the sunny high road. One client of mine is recovering from the death of her mother. During working hours, Vicki carefully focuses on her enthusiasm for a new project. On the weekend she allows her memories of her mom to come into the foreground. That grief is an important part of her emotional landscape, but if given free reign at work it could damage her career. She finds an appropriate time to grieve and makes it a point to use that time. We have choices about what we feel and when we entertain them. Our emotions are not us. When we remember the immensity of who we are, the emotions are more manageable.

There's another tool to help with these emotional choices, the Here-and-Now Wheel. It widens your view of your emotional landscape. The moment you realize you have more emotions, you have more choices. You can choose where you want to be in that landscape.

The Here-and-Now Wheel

This device helps pave the way to our next task, to explore the variety in our mix of emotions. The Here-and-Now Wheel helps me notice feelings I wasn't aware of. It takes me less than a minute, and I can use it twenty times a day, whether I'm overwhelmed by feelings or out of touch with them. I draw a circle the size of a tennis ball

Here-and-Now Wheel
Feelings Right Now

and divide it in four, like a pie. Then I fill the quarters by writing feelings I'm having right here and now, both physical and, emotional.

I then find surprises—such as opposite feelings in the same wheel, like anger and gratitude, sadness and gladness, or despair and hope. The Here-and-Now Wheel helps me pull back the curtain I somehow long ago learned to draw across my emotional world. Sometimes you'll feel a deep sigh when you make a direct connection with your "emotional self."

3) Noticing Our Big Emotional Mix

The Here-and-Now Wheel may already have let you glimpse how vast your emotional variety is. Some languages don't even have names for emotions that other languages easily name. Maybe it's time to start your own list of emotions you have felt. Or just Google "lists of feeling words." (You'll find lots; one I like is posted by Dundee Counselling at https://dundeecounselling.com) Then for fun and enrichment underline feelings already familiar to you, or ones that surprise you, or ones that you usually overlook. Lists of feeling words can help people give a name to their emotions and see how big the mix of emotions is at any moment. You can also get lists from counselors.

For a while, I carried a short list around, small enough to fit in my head for ready use. Some lists are long, a page or more and still not all-inclusive, but long ago I somehow learned the short list: mad, sad, glad, and scared. It helped me get started naming my feelings.

Students of mine used to say, "Hey, that's not fair. Your list has three negative feelings and only one positive feeling."

"Feelings aren't negative or positive," I'd reply. "They're just feelings. They're all there to help us." They weren't convinced, and I knew what they meant, so I now have a slightly larger list to help me and other beginners start owning our emotions: I expanded on the word "glad," with four additional "positive" feelings, one for each letter. So now this "fairer" list includes

Grateful
Loving
Awed
Daring

This could be a start for developing your own feeling vocabulary. If you memorize mad, sad, glad, scared, grateful, loving, awed, and daring, you will have a concise head start on the second step of the Anger-Makeover process, owning your emotions. Each feeling word can bring other feelings to mind. You'll say, "'Mad?' Yeah, I'm mad—and frustrated." Or you'll recall other anger words, such as fed up, annoyed, sick and tired, furious, outraged, or incensed. And you'll have a larger range of words, options personal to you, such as "I'm mad and scared," or "I feel anger, but also so much love and compassion." Just imagine if naming our feelings helped us let go of the option of habitually skirting our feelings and saying, "That jerk!" or any other epithet.

Like my friend Lucy, we would be able to say our true feelings, and never again have to resort to either nastiness *or* silence. Lucy had to take over a badly neglected classroom full of pre-schoolers. As she was beginning to create order out of the chaos, the children at first resisted the change. The more vocal children even said things like, "No, we don't want to stop hitting," and "We don't want to clean up," and "We want our old teacher back."

Lucy didn't tell the children, "You should be ashamed" or "How awful" or "Well, then you deserve to get hurt." She wasn't vindictive. She made no accusations. *And* she didn't just let it go by. Instead, she said with deep feeling, "Well I'm really sad to hear that, because I want you to be safe. I want you to grow up healthy." Her statement was powerful. It's language we could learn to use with people close to us. It was purposeful and personal, helping her stay connected to the people she was addressing. Finding words for your own feelings helps; those words connect you to yourself and to others.

Those three methods may help you with **Step Two, Own Your Feelings**. Once you have 1) written or "scribbled" your reactions or rant, 2) named your emotions (mad, sad, glad, scared, hurt, grateful), or 3) expanded your awareness to include the mix of emotions (maybe with a tool like a Here-and-Now Wheel), you have already created inner change.

All this is not necessarily complicated and can usually be done quickly. In addition, asking yourself some of the following questions may put you more in touch with your inner world of feelings.

- **Have I named or described the emotions I feel?** I can even name the impulse or thought that accompanies my emotion. Sometimes what I feel wants to be expressed, sometimes I get a thought that tells me not to express it. Jotting a note about this may tell me whether my emotion is likely to mobilize me or immobilize me.

- **Have I noticed the physical feelings with the emotions I am experiencing?** Emotions include a physical element. Saying things like "I'm tired," "I feel agitated," or "I feel weak in the knees" can help me get a more complete handle on my emotions.

- **Can I feel the hot spots I have exposed in my writing?** These may be places of pain, anger, loss of control, fear, or worry.

- **Do I suspect even more hot spots, perhaps pieces of unfinished business?** If so, I may want to get them on paper too. Then I can make choices consciously and not let them gnaw at me or overwhelm me.

- **Am I owning my feelings freely to myself first?** There may be emotions I don't like to admit but need to wake up to—before I decide if I want to communicate something to the other person.

- **Have I been able to let my feelings flow on paper?** If I'm in a brassy mood, writing down feelings can help check an explosive flow. If I am feeling more thoughtful or moody, I may need to open up the flow. Then I write to help get off my chest what's lurking there, to sort through some unseen rubble of feelings. Once I write I have a choice. Sometimes I may learn something I don't necessarily want to say or send by accident. Writing can be accident prevention.

- **As I write, am I honoring my insights, feelings, and rights?** Is this a piece of wisdom unique to me that might have gone unnoticed?

- **Looking at what I have written, do I find a place where I stopped the mental lecturing and started owning my emotions?** Did I come more into myself by writing "I feel anger" or "That hurts" rather than endlessly confronting someone mentally? Did I avoid using comments such as "What a jerk," or "You don't know how to do your job," or "Go to ----," or "---- you?" Does writing "I feel sad" feel more powerful or personal than imagining explosive statements or crafting a comeback? When a conflict with someone I know is replaying in my head, do I sense the courage and integrity it would take to say, "I'm angry," or "I feel hurt, or shocked"?

- **Am I surprised that my emotions are worthwhile?** If we typically default to our "timid" side, we may wonder if anyone cares how we feel. First off, it needs to be enough that we let ourselves care. So if you're someone who has typically been silent about your feelings, don't be surprised if you discover that you get people's attention the minute you start being honest about how you feel. Maybe you have already had that surprise, thinking "Oh, my colleagues do care." Or it might be, "My family was moved by what I said." Their acceptance can be scary. Maybe they will take action that upsets your apple-cart. Sometimes the response of people around us is too quick for comfort. We're not used to others taking our feelings more seriously than we have been taking them. Just imagine owning your emotions and getting used to having your feelings taken seriously.

- **Did I explore a variety of feelings?** Feelings in addition to mad—such as sad, impressed, scared, glad, or grateful—we can expand our sense of ourselves. Jenna, a successful middle-aged newspaper columnist, said, "I used to notice only my fury at a driver when the driver pulled out in front of my car." She added, "I sort of missed out on the rest of my experience: my fear, my caring for my kid in the back seat, my gratitude that we survived.

Can I open to the positive feelings too, even while I'm upset? If a friend forgets a lunch date and I feel a bit relieved, can I admit to myself I'm relieved as well as mad? "This happened to me recently," commented Liz, a counselor friend. "I got stood up at a coffee shop. Well, it had lots of magazines for patrons to survey. I caught up on the latest on Janet Jackson. It was just what I needed—a mindless break. In addition, I got to reschedule with my friend afterwards. I learned about his very engaging reason for forgetting the lunch date."

An expressive friend of mine has learned to slow down his more vocal side. That lets him interact with his urges and find what's valuable in them, so he does not let it fly or emote thoughtlessly. If you are one of those who easily express strong emotion, can you notice that emotions often come in layers? Jenna's first reaction was fury. Sometimes the top layer conceals what is below it: gratitude, fear, confusion, or other emotions. Many times, one emotion interacts with another. When we're in a rush of feeling and focused on the obvious, we may not notice the parts.

STEP 3:

WANT WHAT *YOU* WANT. BE SPECIFIC.

Uncovering Your Preferences

This Step Three, what you want, intends to reverse the flaws you identified in Step One, the specific words/actions you didn't want. So here I suggest you call to mind just one of the offensive behaviors or omissions you described in your Step One picture. You may have mentioned several, but to keep this step quick and clear, just focusing on one of the things the person said or did which you didn't like makes it easier for you to write the changes you'd prefer, as well as the possible benefits if the person made those changes. As you go along here, as in the previous steps, pay attention to what's happening in your body, what you feel, and where you feel it. Notice if you feel a different quality of bodily experience, perhaps less intensity or distress and more strength.

1. Write Down the Changes You'd Prefer

Write everything you'd prefer in place of the person's specific offensive behavior. If it's something in the past, what would you have wanted the person to do instead of what she or he did back then?

Your task is to come up with at least one behavior, attitude, or quality you'd prefer in place of the offensive words or action.

Coming up with several preferred behaviors might be even better.

What if the first wishes you write don't feel on-target or specific enough? For example, suppose you feel unsatisfied because you wrote "I want him to grovel," "I want her to improve," or "I want him to get it right." If so, one possibility is that you were in your expressive-only mode and went too fast. Or it could be that you were feeling so reserved that you were hesitant to be clear. You may get a more solid grip on what you want by doing a brief rewrite. You can ask yourself the same question again, or rephrase it as "What do I really want?"

Marshall Rosenberg, PhD, in his *Nonviolent Communication* process (2015) recommends identifying the real need. That too can be helpful. Psychosynthesis counselors working with an angry part, or subpersonality, may suggest first asking that part what it wants, then what it needs, and then what it has to offer. That last question stimulates a transformation. It may be effective to find not just what we want at the moment, but what we want in the long term.

Once you have written the preference or preferences, you can ask yourself the following questions, and then make additions or corrections to strengthen and clarify the preference (or list of preferences):

- **Have I written a "want" that could replace the offensive behavior I described in Step One?**

- **Have I shifted my focus from those outer events to my inner wants?**

Note the switch in this step, from what's wrong with someone *else's* words or actions to an *inner* focus, on what you would prefer.

- **What difference do I experience when I move on to this larger inner focus and its positive possibilities?**

You're also expanding your focus from the negative (things you don't like) to the positive (things you would like instead). For example, I felt distress and anger at governments that kill dissenters, so I ran the issue through the Anger-Makeover process. Thinking about the specific changes I wanted, I became more aware of my wish that these governments would put their efforts into including all factions and trying to work together on their differences and problems.

That expanded awareness inspires me in my own life. Because I have defined these preferences of mine, I have started thinking, for example, of ways I can speak out for social remedies in my own country. The weak position, "I can't do anything about oppressive governments" has changed to a strong position: "There are things I can do."

- **Am I shifting my attitude from "they have to change" to "I have preferences?"**

When we're thinking in terms of "they must," it's a relief to remember words like "I prefer" and "I want." Usually in this step you can practice switching from demands and expectations to preferences. Ask, are there demands or expectations in my Step Three notes that I can release and rewrite as preferences?

We seem to think that if we are angry enough, the other person should get with the program and should get real. Meanwhile, what they may be thinking is that we need to get with the program. We can't change each other by force of will or clenched jaws. Having to make another person fly right is an impossible strain. There's a more effective route.

See whether you experience how deeply effective it is to switch from demands to preferences. Dr. Stauffer described it in her book and workshop on *Unconditional Love and Forgiveness.* Starting in 1973, Edith provided me with early insights that led me to develop the Anger-Makeover process.

If you are willing to pause and look at your demands, you may find them inappropriate. Demands create a power struggle where someone has to lose. (Of course, there is a place for appropriate demands. When someone is assaulting you, you move to stop the attacker. That's another set of skills. This book puts more focus on ordinary situations.)

I had a correspondence with Sister Helen, a Catholic nun in Texas. She and I discussed this tricky problem of expectations. Sister Helen told of another community member, Sister Teresa, who gets frustrated when the community chanting in chapel drags. "She just stops singing," said Sister Helen. "She just sort of sits there and sulks in silence while the rest of the Sisters go on dragging the chant down lower and lower."

This in turn irritates Sister Helen. She also is aware of the dragging, but she loyally struggles at keeping the chant fresh and on key. She wants Sister Teresa's help in this effort. Sister Teresa could be an ally, because she knows how the chant is supposed to sound. She *notices* the others letting it drop off-key.

Sister Helen got relief when she took this issue through the Anger-Makeover process. "I know I'll talk to Sister Teresa when the time is right," she wrote, "but I still occasionally feel thoroughly disgusted." She knew the issue wasn't finished. "Maybe you can tell me," she wrote, "what is still unsolved about my attitudes, expectations, etc."

I wrote back: "You may have put your finger on it already with the word 'expectations.' Feeling solid in your own preferences, your own position, identity, values, beats the powerless position of expecting or demanding that someone else change."

> *"If you're waiting for Sister Teresa to change so you feel okay in yourself, you're giving her the power over your mood."*

You can control your decisions, but not someone else's actions. Your best shot is deciding how you want to influence the other person to control his or her actions. "If you're waiting for Sister Teresa to change before you feel okay in yourself," I suggested, "you're giving her the power over your mood."

Sister Helen's demand style was, "I can't stand Sister Teresa's moodiness." Her feeling was, "She has got to stop getting into a huff and refusing to sing with the group."

"If you pause to notice," I told her, "you'll feel very different when you switch from your inner demand to expressing your position, your wants."

"My preference," Sister Helen wrote back, "would be that she hang in there, keep her cool, and work with me to improve the chant. And that's my position whether she complies with it or not."

What a relief for Sister Helen. This is a change in boundaries—learning to take care of her own emotional yard and let Sister Teresa tend hers. Instead of just dropping her demands and leaving a mental vacuum, she replaces them with a solid feeling about herself and her preferences.

Defining preferences is an exceptionally fine tool in revamping our boundaries and transforming human relationships. I learned from Dr. Stauffer that if, for example, I expect the American Congress to care about America's disadvantaged, I'm dependent on Congress for my feelings of well being. However, if I state it as a preference, I feel the strength and intensity of my own position whether they come through or not.

I can't make them do what I want. I can write or call my Representative. I am more likely to write or call to state my preferences than make demands. I'm less likely to write or call if the point is to demand that Congress change, or if I think my letter or call is a failure whenever Congress doesn't change. It is not a failure. It is another strong example of self-expression. And we usually considerate folks need to learn that our honest self-expression is important in itself—for us and our world. My friend added, "And we usually expressive folks need to learn that a considered response is likely to produce more constructive results than our unmindful outbursts and demands."

- **Can you get clear about your preference and cancel conditions limiting your love for someone?**

Canceling conditions we place on our love is another gift from Dr. Stauffer. Here's an example that might often solve a problem in a common relationship such as parenting. Affirming a prefer-ence instead of restricting your love for someone dear to you can resolve this common but intolerable inner conflict: Our standard impulse of holding love back until someone changes can be psychological and spiritual self-strangulation—while it damages the relationship.

Yes, taking the car keys can be a good consequence for a kid neglecting homework or getting into trouble, but withdrawing love and respect is not. Sometimes when a child misbehaves, parents withdraw love. If they show love on the condition the child behave, they are making something as important as paren-tal love and caring dependent on someone else—the child. Par-ents and kids need the parental love to be unconditional. Appropriate consequences are important; conditional conse-quences like withholding love do more harm than good. All this holds true for any close relationship.

A mother was in a power struggle with her nine-year-old son Mike over keeping his room clean. Using the Anger-Makeover method, she discovered that she was withholding her love for her son to try to enforce neatness. She identified the condition she had been imposing: "Mike, I'll be angry and hold back my love as long as that room is messy."

She later described how, instead of freezing her son out by withholding her love (just as her own parents had done to her), she was learning to work with her son in a warm, loving way. Instead of being harsh and vindictive, she was expressing her preferences clearly and giving him choices with tough conse-quences. "His room's not perfect," she said. "But things are defi-nitely changing—not just his room, but also our feelings for each other." As I listened to this mother, my own heart ached with gratitude to Dr. Stauffer for teaching the importance of the word prefer and letting your love flow.

While working with this mother, I watched the lines of ten-sion leave her face. Tears came to her eyes. Then and there, she opened her heart and let her love again flow to her son. A neat room was no longer a requirement for her love. As her face relaxed, she seemed to be feeling the return of her own motherly creativity and warmth. She decided, "Yes, I want his room clean. It's clearly my preference, and we will come up with a solution, together." When she canceled the condition she had been placing on her love, it was a gift for both of them.

It reminded me of work Dr. Stauffer had done with me in her Unconditional Love and Forgiveness workshop. She helped me correct my thinking about a teacher I was angry with in the school where I was a counselor. The teacher, Cathy, refused to let Craig, a 14-year-old boy, into her class. Cathy was angry at both me and the boy. She hated that I had been hired to replace her friend, the previous counselor, who had resigned and then unsuccessfully tried to get her job back. (All this had happened before I even arrived at the school.) I told Dr. Stauffer I was furious at Cathy for discriminating against the boy. I said I had written her off as inhuman, vindictive.

In the workshop, Dr. Stauffer had me imagine I was speaking directly to Cathy, trying out these words. "Cathy, I'd prefer you respect Craig and help him be successful—and I cancel my demand, accept you as you are, and let my love flow to you freely." I tried it on—and it changed everything. While my preference was solid, I could let go of the mental demand, which, like most of our mental demands, was futile. Already that was a huge relief, but I was still concerned about how Cathy might be deliberately damaging the boy. Dr. Stauffer had me try these words. "And I may have to take steps to restrain you from harming him—while still letting my love flow to you." Although that was not easy, it felt like another huge change. It let me see how love and power don't have to cancel each other out. Preferences come from a combination of good, strong, and skillful will. They include strength. They are not weakness.

• Do I need the other person to change at all?

Is this one of those times when all I need to remember is my own priorities? Example: Samantha works in a printing shop and has a deal with her husband to share housework. It's divide and conquer; when she cooks, he does the dishes. She sometimes feels irritated about her husband leaving dishes in the sink after she has cooked a special meal.

"At first," she said, "I thought I wanted him to do the dishes right away after the meal. Then I defined my preferences and discovered I didn't want that at all. He's a great conversationalist, and we always have a lot to catch up on. I really like spending that colorful, happy time with him after the meal. I prefer he leave the dishes for later."

An awkward or angry situation can have more to do with myself than the other person's behaviors. We think the other person needs to change, but we really need to change our own attitude or behavior. An Anger Makeover sometimes can be useful just for our own clarity. Sometimes we get angry and frustrated and put the blame on the other person, when in reality he or she is doing nothing against our wishes at all. You may have discovered this already in Step One, picturing the problem as you named the behavior you don't like.

By naming specific changes we want in Step Three, we may find out the other person isn't doing or saying anything objectionable. We're fine with him or her just carrying on as usual. It's only a frustration in ourselves or in the situation. We just need to breathe, cool our jets, admit what we really want, and feel our own satisfaction with the way things are. Yes, this may be a bigger problem for you if you are more comfortable with your expressive than your reserved side. You may still just be learning to cool your jets, but that's vital.

I was in a restaurant describing to my friend Hal the first steps of the Anger Makeover. As I was explaining about naming the behavior you want the other person to change, and what you want him or her to change to, Hal appeared to lose interest. He was deep in thought, staring blankly. He pushed back from the table and in a soft voice said very slowly, "You just taught me something. I just learned something. When I say to my wife Charlotte, 'What you're saying isn't making sense to me,' she gets defensive. No wonder: She thinks I'm blaming her. I need to let her know I'm not blaming her. I could say, 'It's not your fault, but I'm having trouble understanding what you mean. It's my fault that I think you should be saying something different. Give me a moment to put on my ears.'" Then he grinned. "And maybe I can ask her to say it in different words that will help me grasp her meaning."

2. Imagine and Write Benefits

Once you have explored the specific *changes* you'd prefer, you imagine the benefits that could result. You find positive imagery. You expand your understanding of the rewards, perhaps for everybody, if your partner or colleague were to make the changes you want. Wishes often feel impossible, but what if they did happen? By imagining them happening, you can change hopelessness into hope. That means you overcome your own refusal to change. I'm not trying to psyche you up to make the impossible happen or to change someone else by sheer, glorious, positive energy. We're simply imagining the best outcome rather than how to make the outcome happen. Later, we may try to influence someone else. Now it's time for a new picture inviting us to change our dream. This takes effort, but if we keep imagining our partner never changing, we are on the wrong side, preventing change. The good news is that any time we catch ourselves imagining the worst, it's in fact an opportunity to picture for ourselves, in full color, how we'd like to see things turn out. A reader commented about powerful effects of using the imagination:

> I love the emphasis on imagery to get out of a mental rut. That is an awesome shot in the arm for me: focusing first on imagining the best outcome, rather than how to make the outcome happen. After all, dieters are often told to love themselves while picturing being healthier and stronger with less weight. Entrepreneurs who succeed in securing capital after hundreds of rejections are supposedly the ones who keep their mind on their idea being successful. I have met two people who have talked cancer out of their body, my aunt, and an overnight nurse I met during my mom's hospice care.

So, for each preference you already listed in Step Three, you imagine your coworker or loved one getting the picture and changing. Then you can list the benefits you'd see, for yourself, your partner, the community, such as more trust, cooperation, or well-being.

The following may be the key to helping yourself with this change in your own behavior. If you want to feel deeply a sense of the good that might result if the other person made specific changes you want, you can ask yourself questions like these.

- **Do I see how important this issue is to me?**

How important is it—or isn't it? How do I now experience the importance it holds for me? And what can I do to remember how important it is?

- **Have I gone all the way with my image of the possible benefits?**

Have I gone ahead and embraced my wishes fully, even if I was afraid I'd be disappointed? What am I willing to do to lock in the optimistic images? If I can even expand on it, might I be less distracted or overwhelmed by the status quo and less likely to give up or shut down?

- **Are there other benefits I can imagine—to myself, my loved ones, or others?**

- **Have I noticed the health in my vision?**

Positive pictures and envisioned benefits have a natural wholeness and validity, just as preferences and values do.

- **Do I let myself feel my pain or grief about the things that aren't happening?**

Is there someone I might want to talk to about these feelings to get a little support with my wish list?

- **What physical relief, relaxation, or exhilaration comes when I stay with my vision?**

What happens in my body when I let my body feel it?

- **Am I willing to continue focusing on the positive image of what I want—and developing it, and projecting it?**

And what if I notice how this feels inside me compared to projecting an image of things I don't like, or worrying about bad things I think might happen? Am I willing to persist?

STEP 4:

ENJOY AND EMBRACE YOUR VALUES

Values and Vision Underlying What You Want

This step goes beyond reflecting on beliefs that generally relate to the issue at hand. Looking at your preferences, you see specific values: things you stand for right now. You may think, "Well everyone must know how important this value is." The reality is that no one else has had the specific learning path your life has given you. So even though we may think everybody already, deep down, holds the values we do, offering ours may reawaken forgotten knowledge or give them something new to think about.

The internal move from preference to value is strikingly quick and powerful. In our example in Section One, here is what June wrote for Step Three, Want Specific Changes: "I'd have preferred that my supervisor Marcie keep me informed about how I was doing during my probationary period."

In June's Step Four, Embrace your Values, she identifies one value. "I think things go better when a supervisor keeps subordinates informed about how they're doing as they go through the probation period." She holds to fairness and information to subordinates. What she prefers and believes in tells us about who she is.

June's process doesn't stop with defining her preference that Marcie consult with her during her training time. It moves to enjoying the value underlying it, her considered belief that it's important for supervisors to help new employees master confusing parts of the job. Yes, if Marcie had warned June about her weak areas, June would have been able to work on them and probably pass her evaluation. It would have been better for all concerned. But the Anger Makeover takes her deeper, to fairness, something June knows deep inside, a profound general principle she holds. That is just a quick step beyond the specific preference.

Fairness is a general principle for many. June is not the only one holding this position. It's a good management principle, so June also finds it natural to say, "Things go better when people are fair to the people under them and deal with them in a cooperative way." In this step June notes that fairness and cooperation are values of hers. It's a direct connection, moving forward from her Step Three preferences. She gains power here by identifying and directly experiencing her values, her core qualities of fairness and cooperation.

As we talked, I could clearly see that these were ongoing values of June's. Even if she had not always lived up to them, she could claim them. We don't have to be perfect to affirm an ongoing value. It's important to remember this as we do this step: A value may still be unquestionably ours, even if we don't always live up to it. Clearly, June didn't believe in telling someone they were doing fine if they weren't. Marcie didn't either. It hadn't been out of malice that Marcie had told June her promotion was in the bag. She just wasn't remembering how tough the rules were that she would have to follow before giving June a promotion. The fact remained that Marcie had made the mistake of telling June the promotion was in the bag and then had withheld it. Later, June admitted that she herself had made even worse mistakes in her life, especially with her small son. Even that didn't mean she had given up important child-rearing core values. Her face broke into a smile at that awareness. While knowing she couldn't be perfect, she was still affirming ongoing values.

You can see from that example how it's a direct move: from wanting specific changes to consciously holding your values, something bigger, heftier. This Step Four can be a rich time of discovery. When I affirm my values, I feel it inside. My back straightens a little, I breathe more deeply, and I remember who I am. I can notice changes in my body and mood. After feeling hurt, I'm feeling whole.

The experience often goes further. I find myself having compassion for the other person, seeing that she or he seems to lack a value that I was somehow lucky enough to get. The compassion softens me. Our values are specific to each of us, coming from a combination of family background, upbringing, life experiences, and who knows what else. But when we remember and affirm what we believe in, affirm who we feel we are, a dramatic switch takes place. After feeling small and desperate, we may feel full-size, not superior, but more generous.

It may be true that June hasn't always lived up to this value. Still, it is her value, even if she had at times slipped or failed with her son—and at times felt regret and self-anger or shame. For thoughts on transmuting excessive shame and self-anger, see pp. 75-90.

It's a Straight Shot from Step One to Step Four

That connection above, between stating your preferences and embracing your values, is a hint to how the first four steps are linked. The Anger-Makeover steps move in a straight line from

One, Feeling provoked by a friend or loved one, to Four, Having more energy and a sense of your own center.

The movement from anger to personal power is direct. You (1) identify the behavior that is irritating you and (2) let yourself feel your anger and other emotions. You (3) go beyond or through the anger to your preference and mentally affirm it. At that point, you (4) discover the inner source of that preference; this lands you in the middle of the garden of values important to you. Sometimes they may be values that you have been taking for granted. You may think, "Of course, everyone knows this." Everyone may not necessarily hold that value. In fact, sometimes we don't quite live up to a value. People may even downplay a value to try to fit in.

Below I've lined up examples from earlier in this book to show the direct line from our anger and dislikes to our preferences and values. Here's what you'll be doing:

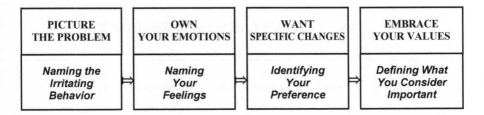

You may first want to experience this for yourself by thinking of your example and filling in the empty spaces in this template:

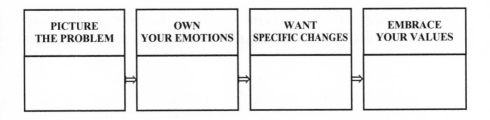

EXAMPLES:
JUNE'S FAIRNESS

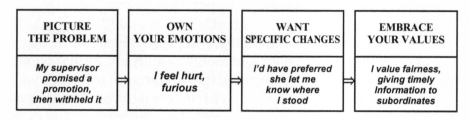

PICTURE THE PROBLEM	OWN YOUR EMOTIONS	WANT SPECIFIC CHANGES	EMBRACE YOUR VALUES
My supervisor promised a promotion, then withheld it	I feel hurt, furious	I'd have preferred she let me know where I stood	I value fairness, giving timely Information to subordinates

SISTER HELEN'S SUPPORT FOR A GOOD CAUSE

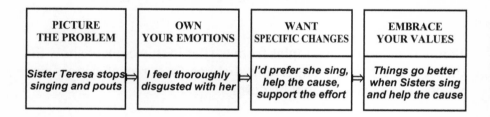

PICTURE THE PROBLEM	OWN YOUR EMOTIONS	WANT SPECIFIC CHANGES	EMBRACE YOUR VALUES
Sister Teresa stops singing and pouts	I feel thoroughly disgusted with her	I'd prefer she sing, help the cause, support the effort	Things go better when Sisters sing and help the cause

ANA MARIA'S CARE, SELF-RELIANCE:

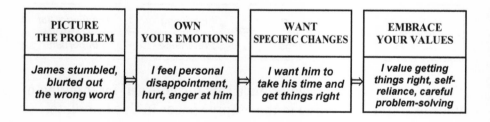

PICTURE THE PROBLEM	OWN YOUR EMOTIONS	WANT SPECIFIC CHANGES	EMBRACE YOUR VALUES
James stumbled, blurted out the wrong word	I feel personal disappointment, hurt, anger at him	I want him to take his time and get things right	I value getting things right, self-reliance, careful problem-solving

Often in a flash Step Four moves you to the heart of your vitality. From there you can renew yourself—and perhaps the relationship.

Let's continue with Step Four. Based on the changes you wanted in Step Three, write a statement of your beliefs—who you are. You can use statements such as, "This is an important conviction I base my actions on" or "Things go better when people…" Then, to help you make additions and improvements, or to enjoy more fully this important step and what it does for you, you can ask yourself the following questions.

- **Is this the value (Step Four) that fuels "what I want" in Step Three?** In other words, does it feel like this value connects directly to my preference?

- **If I were to tell the friend or loved one what I wanted from him or her (Step Three), would it be true to my underlying values or beliefs—or are there perhaps ways to improve my Step Three answer?** Sometimes appreciating a value helps me rethink something I considered set in stone, such as some impulse, stance, or position. If so, I may want to rewrite my **Step Three**. For example, suppose I thought I wanted the other person to shut up and then discovered my underlying value was caring communication. Perhaps this discovery would be a good reason to go back to **Step Three** and revise the want from shut up to a preference such as speak with love and caring.

- **How do my body and spirit respond when I expand my experience from "I want this" (Step Three) to "I stand up for this" (Step Four)?** Is there an expansion in my sense of identity from "I want this" to "This is part of who I am"?

- **If this is truly a belief that may not just benefit me, but also others in the world in general, how willing am I to expand my vision and see that broad benefit?** Is this a universal quality, one that is "transpersonal," potentially of value to every person—past, present, or future? Ana Maria's life may have been changed forever when she embraced her values. At that moment she realized that her belief in keeping one's mind active and awake was something that could benefit anyone who tried it—including her husband, who had not.

- **How does this step help me to believe in myself and not doubt myself?** It's right to care for yourself. That's your responsibility more than anyone's. Let's say you're already good at caring for others, their rights, their dignity. You can continue caring for others and be flexible enough to, in the words of my friend Enid, "include yourself among the ones you care for, honor, and love."

At this point you can check your conviction about the value you're embracing.

If the value is harmful to you or others, your task is to face that squarely and revise it, with professional help if needed.

If the value seems helpful or at least neutral but in the past someone else has ignored or even attacked it, you may have come to doubt it. If so, that needs to be faced. At this moment, how does it feel to say you believe in these values and are standing up for them? And if it's clear that you do believe in them, how do you feel about yourself right now? This step can make a moment—and thus a life—feel less doubtful and more solid.

- **Would I give up these principles?** How important are they to who I am? Am I recognizing and embracing them as values and core qualities of mine? Even soft, warm, and generous values are truly strong. They convey power. Do I find that they are qualities that have long been mine? If these values seem new or are a surprise to me, am I willing to affirm and embrace them?

My values seem close to permanent, maybe eternal. They are at least vital to who we sense ourselves to be now. Could we give them up if we wanted to? A friend said:

> A certain value, efficiency for example, may have been more vital when I worked full time. For those years it may have been very important to my sense of myself. Now that I am retired it may no longer be the value that I once felt it to be. So maybe our

values are who we "are," and maybe they are something we "have." In any case, we experience them as
real and important to us.

- **If I am only now learning to live up to these values, what
  in them do I revere already?** Do I know that no matter
  where I am on my path, these are basic values I hold? It meant
  so much to my friend Daniel to know he could affirm and
  enjoy even shaky values. He had thought for years that because he sometimes went off his diet, perhaps he didn't really
  believe in eating right. He was greatly relieved when he saw
  that he did value eating right—and that honoring that value
  made it more stable and effective. We gain strength by sensing
  our reverence for values fundamental to us. If we let mere
  slips knock our values off the throne, we may let our mistakes
  rule our lives.

- **What do I know about how having learned these beliefs
  and standards may be a gift in my life?** And if I am aware
  that I've gotten a gift, how am I experiencing the awareness—physically, emotionally, mentally, spiritually? Sister
  Helen could see that her fellow Sister sulked instead of doing
  her part to keep the chant on key. Sister Helen said, "I realized, hey, I believe in hanging in there no matter what someone else does. I felt terrific."

- **Do I recognize that lacking these values does not make
  the person bad, and that I was fortunate in getting a *gift*?**
  This is tricky. It's good to recognize that your particular set of
  values is a plus that is unique to you; at the same time, your
  values don't make you superior to someone else. Can you
  imagine what would be missing for you in life if you lacked the
  values you are embracing in this step? I ask clients that question, and they consistently tell me they can't even imagine not
  having them.

After embracing her values, Sister Helen saw just how great a benefit they were. "When I mentally tried to put myself in Sister Teresa's place, it was awful," she said. "I imagined myself getting in a huff and refusing to sing with the choir. I felt really depressed. I could hardly imagine it. I mean, it's part of me: I believe in trying to make the chant sound beautiful. I felt depressed at the thought of being in her shoes." So now instead of resentment, Sister Helen is feeling compassion for Sister Teresa; instead of fear or fragility, she is feeling strength and gratitude.

- **What do I see myself losing if I close my mind to another person's beliefs or values that are complementary to mine?**

The whole world is longing to be understood. Every person needs understanding and compassion. But if "mild-mannered" is your usual routine, remember to listen to yourself too. Feel good about your values.

Feeling good about your values doesn't justify putting the other person down or calling them stupid, bad, inferior, immoral, or a jerk. Notice that your anger is about the person's behavior. You may not know what specific belief he or she is fighting for right now. Why not ask?

Often the other person holds a value similar to yours but is focusing at the moment on a different value. Sister Helen is right in feeling she's lucky in her beliefs. This doesn't mean that Sister Teresa doesn't believe in throwing herself into solving problems too. All we know is that she's not throwing herself into solving this problem in same way Sister Helen is. Sister Teresa certainly doesn't lack values. She may have her focus on some other value, like integrity, saying by her silence that she won't support bad practice. Again, it might be good to ask about or guess at the value underlying someone else's actions—good for you and the other person.

In situations where indulging your silent or mild-mannered

side is your usual routine, it may be valuable for you to get a better grasp on exactly what you dislike and what you like. That's what an Anger-Makeover session can help you accomplish. It may help you feel good about who you are. That might help you show your expressive side more often, enter the discussion, stand up for your beliefs, and speak up for yourself.

Standing up for yourself doesn't equal being condescending, pompous, elitist, or out of touch with the real world. In fact, a new dedication to self-support usually gives you the confidence to be more open to others' values. Now that Sister Helen is confident and clear about not liking Sister Teresa's going on "singing strikes," she can listen to Sister Teresa better. She can listen for Sister Teresa's values and what Sister Teresa thinks she's trying to accomplish by a strike.

The whole world is longing to be understood. Every person needs understanding and compassion. Here's a word or two about situations where you listen to the other person well but hold your expressive side back too much. As a good listener, you may also need to make sure you're listening to yourself. That is what the Anger Makeover is about: listening to what got triggered in you, then what it can tell you about your feelings, preferences, values, options. If you use an Anger Makeover to listen to yourself as you want to be heard, you may find much more effective ways to express yourself. I do. Such listening to yourself and being heard grounds you so you can listen to others better.

And that can help you in situations where you don't hold back your expressive side enough, where you fail to listen to someone. If you turn the Anger-Makeover process around and use it to listen to your coworker or partner as you always want to be listened to, you offer them effective ways to express themselves. That makes your job of waiting easier. For example: Holding back your expressive side a bit and probing for your partner's picture of the issue pulls the person away from their reaction and toward calm and thoughtfulness. Holding your expressive side back long enough to hear a loved one's mix of feelings, preferences, and values may provide them with a whole other calm, rational set of choices about how to talk to you. Wait long enough, and they may even be more ready to listen to you and hear you.

Am I Talking Values Here, or Staking Out a Position?

Let's shine light on the goal of this Embrace Your Values step. Here are **differences between values and positions**. Example: We're driving, and one partner says, "You should have turned. Now we'll be late!" If I'm the driver, I feel royally annoyed and think (but don't say), "Nonsense! I know the way." In such moments, the question is, how can I notice this is a narrow, reactive part of me—and am I willing to get beyond it to a more expanded me? The following is what I've figured out so far. I hope you find it helpful; it seems to help me and make sense to me.

I imagine I'd instantly feel like arguing about the best route—still, I know arguments usually do more harm than good. My immense love for my partner is important. Who needs a frustrating impasse? But where do I go instead? I know that directly underneath my feeling of annoyance and every possible retort lives a value. That is the way to go.

My values are my heartening guides—principles and practices that I have learned, searched, decided on, found important in my life, and loved. In the example, maybe the deeper belief under my annoyance is that I had a good route in mind. By not slowing down to turn, we'd get there faster. So, the value might be competence, effectiveness, or a coherent plan.

When I get a clear picture of my values, I gain inner power, and when I find a way to give that picture to someone close to me, I share my power. Of course, I could automatically blurt out my first impulse—always so imperative, so delicious, so self-gratifying in the moment—and so dreadful later. I feel like stating my position, like, "Oh, come on, that makes no sense." But that's not such a good idea. Our brain locks us into the fear or intransigence or judgment in our reaction—and we spread that. I don't want an argument. Not holding one's tongue at the start is likely to add fuel to a fire no one really wants. And once the fire starts, both sides will likely dig in. That blocks another opportunity to learn something about yourself or the other person that may be surprisingly good to know.

A value tends to expand me, while positions, although they tend to feel concrete and strong, also feel too stationary and a little confining. I would rather expand. If a position is at least nuanced and open-ended it has a better chance at being effective. "I'm not sure your route is better" is a position, but at least it leaves me room to expand. I don't want to rush into a stand that boxes me in.

We end up taking stands for any of a variety of reasons; but most of the time we're jumping into a dispute. That means jumping into the middle of strong (but not thought-out) instinctual reactions. And both sides have those. What we're reacting to felt like a shock or hurt or at least a big annoyance—and usually it felt like some sort of threat.

We have all witnessed a friend or loved one feel a threat and suddenly change. An inner reaction hits them and tells them they're being attacked or offended, and they believe the feeling! "Don't believe everything you think" is a familiar saying. We seldom notice that the belief is just our guess, or our picture of what the colleague or loved one is saying or intending. But that picture may be distorted, as in "Agh! She's trying to control me again!"

We also don't notice that the inner reaction has already taken its stand. We didn't take that stand. It happened before we could think. It's an inward stand already installed by the knee-jerk instinct for self-preservation or preservation of something precious to us. Often we are sure our very dignity or autonomy is at stake. We didn't see that automatically installed stand arrive. It's there. It got there the moment the reactive jolt hit us—blocking the ability of our left prefrontal cortex to calm things and blocking all normal empathy. If we had had a chance to think clearly before our loyal lizard brain took the stand, we'd have found that usually the issue was not safety or survival but a non-issue, a knee-jerk reaction. It was an impulse masquerading as a thought we in fact never thought.

It's just there, seemingly ours. We feel totally convinced *we* rightfully took that stand. We can hardly question it. But in reality, even though it is a big feeling about something small, the stand took us—or a prominent part of us. Primordial distortions that just kicked in that are terribly operative. From centuries of grim practice, those automatic distortions have become all too strategic. They work. We're convinced. In our very gut we know that this specific situation—or rather what we feel is the situation—is a threat. The knee-jerk reaction came in posing as an ally, and with it came already-erected walls of offense or defense. This is how stands or positions invade loving, personal relationships. And unfortunately, the stands last, unless we go deeper, to a warmer, more welcoming place: the value and our calming parasympathetic nervous system.

In political controversies these breakdowns are easier to see—and maybe even harder to counteract. That's why in this beginner-to-advanced book, as you know by now, I don't want us to dwell on political stuff. That can be too big a challenge for beginning stages. A friend said, "I notice that the political discourse bogs down. And it's because the real values are never spoken of—just the positions. The values are implicit, so they go unnoticed by many people."

He also told me something that gives a hint of hope. He noted that one analyst of the American political scene made an assertion: The primary difficulty in modern political discourse is that the opposing sides use the same words to mean different things. So, for example, "family values" means one thing to a conservative and another thing to a progressive. Until a common language of discourse is achieved or agreed upon, no dialogue is possible. That sounds grim but is true. The hint of hope is that each time we do agree upon a piece of common language, dialogue will be possible. And this discussion of "values" may serve that important quest for a common language. If even in the political discourse we are close to achieving that, maybe it's already happening in our intimate discourse with dear friends and colleagues.

I see values as the implied universal principles inside specific positions. The values are always close by, waiting eagerly, but underlying, sometimes out of sight. With loved ones we are often on the brink of getting mired in the quicksand of contradicting each other. But when I can pause to let myself see the values clearly, the values help me—and potentially help the friend or loved one I might have pushed away when I would jump into another stance.

So when I remember to unearth an underlying universal value during a conflict (or even after the conflict), a mindful pause gives me space for the Anger Makeover. I am rethinking the feeling or particular impulsive stance or comment that snuck in and may still be ruling the roost in my head. This is the crucial move to make: the switch from "what I think, demand, or want" to some deeper, calmer level of "what I value." This is at the heart of the Anger-Makeover process. It's what moves my attitude from anger to personal power.

Bear in mind that it may still not be enough just to discover my value, such as "I trust the route I'm taking". Although the discovery may change my attitude and reduce my arousal, that doesn't necessarily tell me what to say. I am just in a clearer state, so I can pause, relax, and choose from new and better options. The options may include also squeezing in a guess at my partner's underlying value, such as "Yes, we believe in getting there on time." And this gets even better. Suppose if in the same breath I can also squeeze in that value of mine, "I'm trusting the route I'm taking to get us there on time." That's a pair of values that begs for synthesis.

On occasion, after a thoughtful inspection of values, I may even go back and change a position I had taken. I may see more clearly that the impulse was merely an urge to prove I was right. Replacing the impulse may effectively dissolve my belligerent stance. People's impetuous feelings of "I'm right" or "You're wrong" spark many quarrels in loving relationships—enough to eventually destroy many relationships. But who's right is seldom important, no matter how urgent the impulse feels. My instinct to be right is an attempt to be safe. That is unnecessary because I already am safe. (If not, I need to seek serious help.)

I'm not saying there's no such thing as right and wrong, good and evil. It's just that too often a dramatic, reactive impulse convinces me that something fairly unimportant has become terribly important. I'm safe already and don't need to be right, especially right now. Those instincts are designed to absolutely demand instant action—otherwise they'd be useless for real survival. For me, instant action usually makes things worse. In a crisis, instant action is life-saving, but most of our lives happen at work and home without any real crises. The absolute demand for instant action gets in the way of equal, respectful exchanges.

When something challenges my beliefs, I feel instant annoyance. And Mr. Annoyance likes to argue, even in jest. I'm even examining my humorous play arguments. The banter can be fun, but when there's a hurtful hook hidden in this play, even if unintended and unnoticed, that hook may hurt my beloved play partner's heart, or mine. It's a sad risk, one I'm experimenting with skipping. I'm challenging myself with a playful alternative: mentioning a value I like on the loved one's side.

When we can't understand why it seems to us that a friend or loved one morphs before our eyes into a lethal combatant, it's easy to grab verbal weapons and forget all the delightful verbal tools available. Self-defense when there's no real threat is an old habit, and it's offensive. When I defend my positions, quarrels are more likely. And of course the one morphing is often me.

To sum up, values are broader to me, while positions are specific and pricklier. Values are guiding principles that my more central self has gathered and refined over years. They are rich, representing a deeper, long-term level of consciousness. And because values are more universal, not exclusive to your side or my side, they are less likely to spark hostility. Instead, they encourage constructive work. They are potentially much more inviting and compelling to a friend or loved one who is having a difference with us. Our values take us to a whole other realm. They are not just personal; they are transpersonal, potentially spanning the consciousness of many persons. That gives them more positive influence—if I remember to embrace them, and, when appropriate, state them. Stating a value even just inwardly to myself in a personal relationship, especially from a warm, calm place, may in turn invite the friend or loved one to share a related value. Speaking at the level of values leads us to that common language we're trying to find. And it is more likely to invite mutual respect: We both keep becoming more and more right.

Since finding your own values is so helpful, imagine what happens if loved ones in a conflict are also willing to seek out each other's values and embrace them. Then, the couple sets in motion magical surprises: new combinations that have a life of their own. These new directions are satisfying to both and benefit both. They embody a set of values from both people, so an either-or controversy turns into a both-and collaboration.

For me, this switch away from a fight can be very hard. My reptile gut loves a fight. And knee-jerks don't care if it's stupid. But the switch is easier once I know that a sharing process promises something exponentially richer. I'll be standing on a new platform, one that's not so narrow but in fact much broader.

So, what about our example where I've driven past the turn point? Suppose I respond to my partner's comment with a couple of values I think we share. "We both want to get to our destination on time, and I think this route will get us there on time. It's too late to take that turn, but I hope you can trust me here. If this doesn't work, I'll take your route next time. Will that be okay?" Maybe something like that would invite discussion instead of argument.

STEP 5:

REVIEW YOUR RANGE OF OPTIONS

Realistic Words and Actions

By now, you've discovered useful things in Steps One through Four. You have a more specific picture of the problem. You are aware of a whole mix of emotions. You see specific changes you'd prefer. You can feel the power of the values underlying those preferences. Step Five is the time for exploring all this new territory. Just by reviewing what you've written, you see that you have more options for responding to the situation or person that troubled you. True, there's still the old option of suffering from the anger and stress, or enjoying it too much. But the tension has probably gone down. You're no longer caught in it. You're freer. You now have a rich array of feelings and actions to pick from, from reserved to expressive. Here again, as options occur to you, pay attention to how each one moves your body, what you feel, and where you feel it. For example, some may feel right and solid in your spine, or arms, or trunk. Some may feel less right physically than others.

Sometimes when I'm going through the Anger-Makeover process, I start this Step Five review by just going back through what I've written in the first four steps and circling everything usable. While I corral these options, I keep an eye out for the moves or statements I know would be kind and respectful of the other person. Then I open to this hearty, goodwill side available to me for any additional ideas that might be percolating—options that might be constructive—and, yes, kind. Kindness in a conflict, you ask? "Kindness itself," says Piero Ferrucci (2007), "might seem lightweight, and yet it is a central factor in our lives. It has surprising power to transform us, perhaps *more than any other attitude or technique* (emphasis mine) (p. 11)." Our goal is to transform ourselves and our performance, not the other person.

In this step, we're still deliberating. We're not usually far enough along to be planning what we are going to say, or be, or do. It helps to stay loose now and think, "Before I decide, let me make sure I have a full array of possible tools out where I can see them." We want to expand our thinking here and not miss great, sometimes still unfamiliar, possibilities.

Deliberating beats snapping to one of those two old, tired options of shutting down or yelling. On the one hand, when I'm in a mode of staying too reserved, my problem is I think I'm staying safe but may just be sitting on my irritation until I can't keep a lid on it—then ending up yelling anyway, or saying something that is barbed with favorite passive weapons of mine, such as sarcasm or implied blame. On the other hand, when I'm in a mode of overusing my expressive side, it may feel great to just blow up. But blowing up may be too handy an option—I might take it before giving myself time to think.

Avoiding both those extremes in our relationships is so important. Our objective in "**R**, Reviewing Our Range of Options," is to eliminate all passive and aggressive weapons and look for reserved and expressive tools. Our psychological tools have heart, caring for others and self.

Looking over how you responded in the first four steps typically gives you a bunch of better options. Now, once you have opened to those ready options, and to any additional ones that come to mind, here are a few questions to help you explore and evaluate what you've got.

- **Have I let myself freely brainstorm?** The idea in this step is to let in all the ideas that come to you, no matter how wild, creative, crazy, sensible, or outrageous at first sight.

- **Do I notice heartfelt options in Steps One through Four?** Have I highlighted all the worthy ideas?

- **Are there good sides to old bad options?** Even seemingly useless habits can be repurposed or combined with new ideas. If I've been overusing the option of saying nothing in conflicts, I might still contemplate saying nothing, but now study possible good and bad effects. My old bad options are certainly worth considering for possible new workable modifications and combinations.

Also, the habit of not saying anything might be modified to a healthy habit of pausing before speaking, just long enough to choose a conscious direction. For example, here is a small step that Terri, long married, could take with a tedious problem. She comes home to find the sink filled with her husband's lunch dishes when she wants to prepare dinner. Before she does anything else, if she needs to hold back her frustration, her first step past silence about bad feelings could be to talk about good feelings. If she still doesn't want to tell her husband how ticked she is when it happens, she can start thanking him whenever she finds them done—and let him know how nice it is to start her meal preparation with a bright, clean sink.

How about if your problem is the opposite habit, saying too much or sounding off before thinking? Ironically, this too can be modified to a healthy habit. You pause long enough to choose a conscious direction before speaking. We may decide it is still a good move to voice our anger about dirty dishes once again holding up the cooking, but we could do it in a consciously measured way, even just using a word like "disappointed" or "slowed up" instead of "angry." That alone may get helpful attention and not just provoke an equal and opposite reaction. And here too, a first step in expressing these feeling could be to pause, then move on beyond voicing bad feelings to talking a little more about good feelings. With a short pause, you may find a hundred gentle ways to make your point.

- **What energy change do I get from simply imagining using an effective option?** Sometimes after going through an Anger Makeover, I get energy and strength just thinking of saying something that before would never have occurred to me. June said, "I felt my spine straighten when I got the idea that I could write a letter to be included in my file at work beside that bad review. I realized it would not only counteract the bad review but even let me lay out my ideas about improving the performance-review process. The moment I decided to do it, it was like my energy came back."

- **Can I imagine solving a problem when I don't agree with someone?** Imagine the shift from wanting to turn someone off, even be rid of someone, to wanting to build something, even mend a fence together. If I kept in mind the possibility of creating or re-creating an alliance, it might be easier to decide which options to use. Or instead of delivering a correction in a one-way blast, can I imagine scenarios of a two-way interchange, with me using options from my expanded list?

GAINING FULL
ANGER-MAKEOVER BENEFITS

Imagine and Choose Realistic Action

Okay, an Anger Makeover has transformed my inner feelings: Now that I feel stronger and calmer, how can I restore good feelings with the colleague or loved one?

Yes, finishing those five steps was inner work. So, in the outer, real world, what's next for this relationship? In other words, now that you feel grounded and have found the gold hidden in your gut reactions, what now? Here is an action midway between personal inner work and an external, real-world conversation.

You can start now with direct, heartfelt internal interactions. You can mentally talk to the friend. This may sound imaginary, something only for when you are uncomfortable actually talking or want to practice what to say. But practiced communications are not just inner work within yourself. In reality, internal, mental, or spiritual statements can exert energies that are subtle yet real, powerful enough to connect. By trying them out, you get to see how they change the relationship.

Our thoughts not only grow our neural pathways, they grow relationships. Even before you feel comfortable enough to speak directly to someone, you can see how thoughts directly affect the relationship. By just thinking and mentally saying how thankful you are for the other person's friendship, love for you, patience and forgiveness, service to you, or anything else you appreciate, you're communicating, saying a prayer, or giving a blessing.

You can also mentally say what you feel, or prefer, or believe. Even if you don't expect such mental actions to reach the other person, you can try them. You may see how they immediately benefit you and your bond with the loved one. Even if you have serious concern about a friend's mistake or malfeasance, that does not have to eclipse your enthusiasm and gratitude for the essence of who they are. The enthusiasm and gratitude are still real. You can be the gratitude and lovingly hold the concern within the gratitude.

The genuine, solid benefits and joys in your relationship are real. It would be sad to drop them completely if you can keep them. The sooner you can wholeheartedly treasure these well-earned benefits and joys, the better. You may want to put your deep appreciation into words. Appreciation doesn't cancel out ways you and a colleague or loved one are different. Nor do your differences need to cancel out your appreciation. You may be able to keep a relationship that, although fraught, benefits you and your loved one.

If you're willing, you can try mentally communicating any of your appreciations and see for yourself. Or you can try mentally communicating any of the ways you are different from your associate. You can tell them any of the preferences that showed up in an Anger Makeover. There is a spiritual side of us that is already and always aware, powerful, and nonjudgmental. We can access that Self and experience being it actively. It's who we are. And when we can be that spirit while embracing our other knowings, feelings, preferences, convictions, imagery, reactions, and desires, we can move forward in a uniquely personal way. We can profoundly change a relationship conflict by mentally speaking from our best Self.

You can do any of the above any time in your work with the Anger-Makeover process. The mental communication helps you avoid setting in stone your judgments, bitterness, accusations, or raw anger. By underlining your nonjudgmental appreciation, love, and positive values, you become stronger and more yourself.

Combine inner reflection with actual discussion and action. Even after saying all this, we have to decide about what to say or how to act. We have to choose to act in a certain way or not to act. Even though the above transitional work already changes things in the real world, we may want to do more. Yes, our mental or spiritual communication may affect us and our loved ones in multiple ways, but it may feel right to extend the inner changes, to connect them to our relationship in person, one-on-one. By interacting physically we can make our work more effective. So once we have finished an Anger Makeover and perhaps communicated mentally or spiritually, it remains for us to decide what to do in this other world, the world of visible social interaction where we feel our feet on the ground.

Your results from an Anger Makeover give you power. By stopping and evaluating your anger, you've gotten new data. You've respected your emotions, listened to them. You have new power and new options—a range of possible moves, expressive and/or reserved. Now, if you can feel this new power as an opportunity, how else can you use it? What you do with this can make a difference.

You're set for all kinds of inspired, imaginative action. Your good inner learning can lead to good outer, empathic action. So the whole picture changes. No need to rush into or stay in a battle, or sit and stew, or wrestle with replays, or be stuck. No need for that outdated pre-armed, even pre-peeved defiance. You make room to explore possible creative interactions with the colleague or loved one. Anger Makeovers are first about mindfulness and feeling your way through. This happens in your body, within yourself. Once you've done that, you're more ready to work with the other person.

So, once you have used your imagination, you can take action when you judge it appropriate. Below are a few suggestions to think about now, while in a relaxed state. They're constructive options for when you're fired up and ready to interact instead of react. You might end up simply imagining sitting down with the other person long enough to calmly tell your appreciations, or share a value from your Anger Makeover. You'd be listening to a loved one and imagining where it goes from there.

Your inner work will definitely be felt in your outer words and actions. And you'll take another step in improving pathways in your brain and making your work in the world easier. I predict that if you try three or four of the following suggestions before you say or do anything you will be able to communicate more effectively from now on.

Recall When Someone Was Mad at You. What Did You Want and Not Want From That Person?

When you consciously remember a time when the shoe was on the other foot, you know what kind of treatment would you have wanted from the person that was mad at you. At a workshop in San Francisco I asked people to go back to a time when a person had confronted them and recall how it felt. "Say one word or one sentence indicating what you would have liked," was my request. "What quality would you have appreciated as someone expressed anger to you." These are the verbatim answers:

I would have appreciated . . . a sense of interaction

> . . . if I had been received with understanding compassion.

> . . . kindness and honesty.

> . . . not being branded a criminal but being trusted—and that the person had let me know in the beginning instead of at the end.

I would have liked for the other person to listen to my side of the story.

> . . . the other person to have continued to include me in the relationship.

157

. . . a heart connection when they were interacting with me.

. . . Respect.

. . . that it was my behavior they were angry at, and I wasn't being labeled as bad.

I would have preferred

. . . that my side would have been listened to, and I had been given the opportunity for interaction . . . . interaction towards reconciliation.

. . . acceptance of me even though they were angry.

. . . respect for my person.

. . . that she showed me how sorry she was instead of how angry she was . . . her sadness.

Remembering your longings at such times could change what interaction you move to from your internal Anger-Makeover process. You might want to start your own list of ways you want to behave, by noting what you want from other people when they're angry at *you*. That's right: Think about your communication plan in the light of what *you* would want. Here's the trick, once you catch an anger reaction in yourself: pause, and do an Anger Makeover. This does take practice. Oh, yes, I recall times I wish I had done this but was too caught up in the conflict. It would have been better to take the break. Using the Anger-Makeover process I can still, always, go back and break down old grudges. I can end my unending battles.

When our nice person side makes us go silent, we often end up stuck in the anger. People who typically don't speak up in conflicts may have *great* things to say. In an altercation, they may just need to become familiar with ways to be respectful, courageous, and creative. Humans can master the ability to behave in ways the workshop participants above said they'd appreciate, such as maintaining a heart connection, not stay stuck in anger.

(Oops, I just remembered someone I'm judging in anger. I've gone silent on him. Time for me to have another 5- to 20-minute Anger-Makeover session with myself.)

A silent pause is sometimes the right strategy, but not permanent silence as the usual practice. Better to start trying new things, with conscious care. With a little Anger-Makeover work, we don't have to go through life just dropping issues and never bringing them up at all—any more than we have to go through life showing other people our unchecked emotion. In our respectful, loving relationships it might be better to explore ways to invite discussion.

And now a word from the expressive-aggressive camp, a friend of mine who feels he is too inclined to use his expressive side. He commented that the Anger Makeover is not just good when we are too slow to speak up.

> Equally, when we who are usually quick to express anger allow ourselves to let fly, we are equally stuck. The unthoughtful reaction cuts off constructive responses, and it provokes reactions instead of solutions. A pause really helps. Sometimes I need to take a half-hour walk, and by the time I return I have had time to try on different thoughts, put the other person's shoe on for a moment. I use the Anger-Makeover process to tap into a deeper part of me.

He's right. It might be good for those of us who typically favor our brutally honest side to keep in mind how misleading that pair of words can be. We think both words carry the same weight, but in brutally honest the "honest" is a throw-away. To the friend hearing us, we just come across as brutal. Especially with long-time friends and loved ones, once we must start monitoring those powerful instinctual reactions. We don't have to live out our lives as curmudgeons cutting off their communication or making yet another pronouncement. We can find much better things to say.

My friend above found a perceptive quote from Timothy Pina, author of the children's book *Bullying Ben*. "An ounce of kindness always goes a lot further than an ounce of bitterness. So sprinkle it every time you can. You always can." That "always" is empowering.

Voice Your Respect First: Right Away. Before Your Preference.

Respect is part of the plan. Let's establish that and explore ways to experience our respect and put it into action and words. Think of one thing the person did right, or recall *any* of the many things you appreciate about the person—you can even get your thanks into your introduction right off the bat.

Keeping true collaboration in mind, I recall something my late colleague and friend Dr. Ken Wells recommended. He was director of the Counseling and Psychotherapy Institute in Albuquerque, New Mexico. He said, "Write a letter to the person you are blaming, thanking that person for all the good things he or she has done for you. In it you will also apologize for the ways you may have made him or her uncomfortable." If that bit of writing were done before, during, or after every confrontation, it would change the tone of the confrontation, and this world wouldn't be divided into so many warring camps.

As head of Psychosynthesis International in California, Dr. Stauffer often had the angry person just write down everything he or she appreciated and valued about the other person. "Do that for one month," she said, "before saying anything. Then tell the person the positive things. But you have to be honest," she adds. "You can't make things up."

She said that everyone that has tried this suggestion has noticed that before the month is out, the other person is starting to change for the better. This practice of hers fits well as a follow-up to an Anger Makeover. A friend of mine even upped the ante, with his comment.

> This is so important. I have experienced this many times. When I have made a substantial change in my own attitude toward another person, before I

confronted them, I have found that when I see them again their behavior has already changed on its own. Not always, but many times. So it turns out that taking a pause myself, and also allowing the other person time for a pause, sometimes allows something to happen beneath the surface that eventually shows positive results.

Another more-expressive reader agreed. "This power of not expressing one's strong opposite feeling seems very beneficial for expressive folks, because it doesn't put the other person on tilt, or maybe makes them feel heard."

Accordingly, before I talk with a friend or loved one about a disagreement, I first need to get far enough past the knee-jerk reaction to re-establish my respect and appreciation and lock it in. And I need to join forces with them to maintain the good feelings. Also, it's good to know that as we grow, our goal can be better attitudes toward even wrong behaviors of coworkers or loved ones. We don't want punishment, but instead a clear stand or differentiation. When possible, we want to prevent harm.

The fact that you're reading this book already says you know you can create new habits. They must include the habit of staying dedicated to your rights, feelings, vision, and self-respect. That lets you respect the other. As soon as you see a conflict, you can call for a pause. "I see we are going to disagree. I respect you and me, and I'd like to pause." Then you can make a request tailored to your situation. It might go something like, "Before we go further, can we discuss whether we're both willing to love and respect each other enough to rule out anyone on either side getting blamed, shamed, or yelled at? We can certainly rule out anyone making or allowing accusations, judgments, or disrespect." Lacking that kind of collaboration, it might be best to change the subject.

Here's something it took me years to learn: In conflicts, when I open my mouth I need to consistently, first of all, speak from my nonjudgmental Self, and then, speak up for the preferences and values being guarded by the part of me that's disagreeing.

On one occasion during the COVID-19 pandemic I spoke badly, but I recovered and learned a lot. I felt very disappointed when an Australian friend I admire sent me poorly done videos of COVID conspiracy theories. I found them fake, even bizarre. Talking with her on Zoom afterward I said, "Carla, when you buy in to that stuff, I lose respect for you."

I saw her look go dark—and unbendable. I later recognized I had expressed a judgment coming from a disgusted part of me. It certainly had not been my discerning and nonjudgmental spiritual Self speaking. I realized that I could have just skipped judging and disparaging her position and instead expressed respect for her, along with my preference. In fact, doing that is vital and much needed today. I could have freely, fully respected her and freely, fully disagreed with her and her opinions, which to me seemed puzzling and irresponsible.

The next time we talked, I first of all apologized for judging her. I very simply told her about my respect and love, as well as my preference that she not send such clips. I had used a brief Anger Makeover to get clear about that. I'm still too appalled to explore her values and pursue synthesis, but at least I mindfully expressed high regard for her, which for multiple reasons I still feel. It took some inner struggle, but I honored my love for her while also honoring my strong value of caring for people's lives.

Some part of me asks: But isn't there something wrong with this so-called synthesis? To be "respectful," didn't you have to ignore your own sense of truth and morality?

I think this question means If I thought Carla was naïve and being hoodwinked by conspiracy-theory wackos (which I do) and if I thought her attitude was immoral in that it spread the virus (which I do), how could I not fight her to debunk her ideas? (See the discussion of moral convictions on pp. 26 and 27.)

I don't see the approach of impulsively fighting family or friends and debunking their notions as my job or a good idea. It's not even practical, and is unlikely to work. In a situation like that I am willing to say, "I don't want to argue about what you just said, but I wouldn't want to be silent and have you assume my silence was consent. I would be willing to talk sometime, provided we can agree on a two-way goal, like for us to understand our differences."

I didn't have to ignore my truth in order to be respectful and not fight. First, I had tried fighting. Predictably, it had only made her more stubborn. That's the usual outcome from arguing and attempting to dominate or make someone change.

Second, a principle came to mind I learned long ago studying the philosopher and theologian Thomas Aquinas. "The individual conscience comes first." It meant that Carla was the only one who had authority over her decisions—all of them. I didn't agree with her, and I'm deeply disappointed at her choices, and I wished she had better discernment and I could change her, but I remembered that she alone can, and must, decide her course. Always. This shows that she, like all of us, needs to exercise careful insight about her beliefs. Only she can decide. She has a responsibility to behave in accord with her best lights.

Welcoming Others' Conscientious Differences

I do not claim to be good at this. The part of me that wants to fix others' thinking is in the way. Yet I believe that when we learn to honor that principle, welcoming conscientious differences of others, it will sweep away tons of arguments and debris and bring change. Imagine how day-to-day differences, and maybe conflicts in the larger world, will change when a few more of us remember this. For every single one of our loved ones and friends, what trumps all options for them is what their individual conscience tells them to do. As soon as we remember that, respect will flood the arena of relationship conflict.

Certainly, we will still have conflicts. They are not necessarily something bad. But they will be different. We will still hash out differences, but as honored peers. Of course, we may fail to get them hashed out. Carla and I failed at it. It was, after all, a very political issue. I saw little point in trying to share my values, since she wasn't listening, but in fact was in an ardent proselytizing mode. It didn't seem like a good use of time.

Still, many of us might learn to show more respect in conflicts with family and friends—and when necessary, change the subject. I've since made more use of the Anger-Makeover process to uncover the energy and values underlying my anger at Carla for sending out those lame COVID conspiracy theories. However, I didn't do it to share the results with her, but to get more clarity and growth for myself.

She and I can always choose to go back and explore ways we might be able to compare notes, if we're willing to understand each other's preferences and values. Meanwhile, we still get to enjoy being peers with precious common interests. In our case, being peers beats ending up as former associates walled off and distant forever. It is especially important for couples, friends, and family members to know when not to feel morally obligated to correct or prove each other wrong, righteously turn our backs, or settle into resentment.

Remembering to honor Carla's responsibility for her actions dramatically reduced the strain inside me and between us. Applying pressure had been worse than useless anyway. In any conflict, not only must each of us freely follow our own conscience, not the preference of an idol or spouse or friend, and make our own decisions. We also need to insist on that freedom for each other.

Where does this discussion leave us? We have an opportunity to explore how we're each different; to stay open to a better understanding of each other's preferences and deep, positive values; and to see a bigger picture. There even remains the opportunity, if we learn to cooperate further, to polish the opposite positives and put them together into another new synthesis.

Dignity for Both

I'm recalling the warning, "Live by the sword, die by the sword." Any exchange short on *equality* and *intact dignity* ends up wounding both your partner and you. Impulsive "putting him in his place" or "fixing her little red wagon with square wheels" is living by the sword. You get to die by the sword, or take another wound, or lose a relationship. The issue, at least, is not resolved. And chances are that if your friend comes back with yet another knee-jerk reaction, the war, cold or hot, is back on.

My comments about respect in the above section recommended starting a dispute on the right foot with honest appreciations for your partner. This dignity section here is about keeping it an honest two-way exchange that upholds everyone's dignity. That requires full participation. You may think you are keeping the peace by skimping on information or honesty. But if your associate or friend is honest and puts themselves out there and you don't, besides shorting yourself, you may be seen as putting the other person in a compromising position or being patronizing.

Readers of this book who are usually peacemakers rather than warmakers may find it easier to preserve equality and dignity. Impulsiveness may possibly be less a danger for them. However, the risk they run is clamping too heavy a lid on their own thoughts and feelings. They need to watch for damage they may do by passive, cold-war habits—behaviors they don't even notice they're using to drive someone else bananas. These include not responding, turning away, procrastinating, repeatedly coming late, and so on. Or they're silent and nice when a loved one needs them to be forthcoming and honest about preferences and values, if not feelings.

A stark example of this need for reserved people to be sometimes more courageous and honest came from a highly expressive friend of mine.

> My mother was the passive-aggressive type who was so nice she would not say "s--t" if she had a mouthful. Her behavior not only enabled bad behavior in her family, it actively provoked it. And one could never confront her, because she would just get nicer—and then cry. She was even more disruptive to family harmony than my over-the-top-expressive angry father: He was hard to approach, but he could be approached— very carefully. But we could not overcome her timidity and niceness, and we all hated it. It masked intransigence. It was very destructive, and in the end it

isolated her more than my father's rages isolated him. So it is vital that the hesitant person be willing to use the Anger-Makeover process to come out of the shell and negotiate. This takes courage.

Am I Stalling . . . or Planning?

What's nice is that the often-maddening tendency to stall can also be a strength: the ability to wait. Waiting, as a tool, can be absolutely vital—especially if we use the waiting time to calm down, use the Anger-Makeover process, and plan a strategy. Then we're not avoiding contact but getting ready for it. Instead of indulging our mindless reflexes, we can look in our conflict toolbox for reserved or receptive tools that soften our face and voice, tools for crafting constructive interactions. Some of us are experts at the ability to wait. That's a tool resting in there with other reserved tools—one that's especially effective when we combine it with an expressive or communicative tool such as an invitation to compare ideas.

Our purpose in waiting is not to put the issue on ice forever. We need to move forward whenever possible with mutual respect and cooperation. And as soon as we hatch a respectful plan, ideally together, the challenge is to work our plan.

It's a big challenge, perhaps impossible unless we remember to use our imagination. Once you can imagine carrying out the plan with dignity, respect, clear boundaries, and purpose, you can take action or talk about it. You might say, "Oh! Good point. So, essentially you're saying . . ." The exchange may not come out perfect, but we need to stop demanding perfection—of ourselves or each other.

Gratitude and Deal Making: Pulling Together Dissimilar *Plusses*

The big problem with arguments is you can't homogenize people: We will never be the same. We won't think or believe the same. So, it's good to consciously differentiate with reverence: spell out our differences and perhaps enjoy them—and the benefits we hope they'll bring. Accepting the ways we're different is the essential first step toward synthesis.

So instead of getting sucked in to instant argument we could encourage respectful, purposeful interaction. Before we talk, we could find agreement on the sort benefits we both want from the discussion: maybe the kind of conduct and outcomes we'd both like—such as seeing how we're different, finding the different ways each of us is right—and working to combine the positive differences.

In Roberto Assagioli's book *The Act of Will*, the founder of Psychosynthesis showed how this goes beyond the mutual dilution strategies of compromise (get-something-lose-something). It can lead to something new and richer: synthesis. He said, "Two elements are absorbed into a higher unity endowed with qualities which transcend those of either" (1999, p. 101). He used a triangle to illustrate this upgrade. For example, in a conflict between two opposites, being excited or depressed, the compromise might give calmness, whereas by combining the positive values on both sides we might achieve serenity.

Let's bring this down to earth. Synthesis could relieve many a domestic squabble. Singly or together, we can look for the values on one or both sides. That can replace arguing about who is right. In fact, with or without my partner, I can change the frame to one of cooperation, or rebuilding, or solidarity, or exploring of positive values. Quickly, everything from both sides feels and sounds better. Your initiative can make the difference. You can prepare yourself before a discussion, using the Anger-Makeover process. Once you've done that, you can share pretty much any of your material from the first four steps, provided you're careful, vulnerable, and honest.

You don't have to do it all yourself. Helping the other party explore with you reduces barriers. This sort of do-it-yourself therapy may take some guts, but if it makes sense to you, try it. Of course, you'll tailor your material to the unique person and situation. You wouldn't say to your mother or grandmother what you might say to a long-time buddy. But no matter who I'm with, being armed with the Anger-Makeover process makes it easier to talk clearly. It changes everything, having in reserve the raw material of any ideas you already came up with in those first four steps.

My friend Dan, a therapist, nicely articulated the age-old false dilemma. "When someone gets mad at me, I have the immediate feeling of 'I must have done something wrong.'" He paused, then added with a fierce grin, "Three days later, it's 'Well, he's the jerk!'" He sighed, "I wish I could come up with a clear response in the moment, without first being devastated." A clear response is possible in the moment or soon, if you stop and remember the five Anger-Makeover tasks. By the way, they can also work when the reactions are flipped, whenever you feel the coworker was the jerk and then later realize it was you in the wrong.

If we're inclined to favor our reserved side in conflicts, we may need to support ourselves sooner, especially in our long-term relationships. But it needs to be without name-calling, even in our heads. I told Dan I feel more powerful when I can be specific about what the loved one did or said that offended me.

Nothing works for every situation or person, but a wise young woman offered me some emotional-self-defense moves. One could say, "That hurt, and I feel angry," or simply "Ouch!" If your partner said something emphatic and insulting, you could say, "That's what *you* think." But here's a warning another friend offered about care with your words.

> Sometimes I notice that any kind of expression of anger provokes a defensive reaction in some people. Even just saying it like that ("That hurt, and I feel angry"). Assagioli cautioned us against approaching some issues (and some people) head-on. When dealing with some people, maybe it is a good strategy to explore alternative ways to approach them and work our way up to the place where saying "I'm angry" can elicit constructive engagement instead of either defense or attack or flight.

I've noticed the same. To my mom in her middle-American farm world, direct expression of anger in simple words would have felt foreign and harsh, as it still might to me. So what are alternate approaches? In situations where I usually get too quiet, I have an approach that would certainly get my friend or loved one's attention: telling them simply what I want or what my values are.

At the times when we're usually more reserved, we sometimes hoard a lot of information about how we see the situation. Leaking a few specifics might go further than we ever imagined. For example, we could say a bit about our view, or our pain, or our confusion, or what we'd prefer. And can you imagine if we were to list one or two of the possible benefits the person could bestow on us by simply doing one thing we've said we'd prefer? For example we might say, "If you slowed down just a bit, it would help me relax a lot." But we may first need to tell ourselves our preferences or values, before we speak out loud. Speaking is easier once we do an Anger Makeover.

So, what approaches do you think might improve your situation? There may be times a friend or loved one has a right to know what you're thinking and feeling about a question. You of course might need to wait a bit to think and rehearse. And later you may have more time to discuss it and let them in on your inner world.

Enjoy the New Clarity and Confidence

An Anger Makeover readies you to be more effective in what you say. You've paused and worked inside yourself. You've thought through the conflict in simple steps. True, sometimes it is good to wait when someone has offended us and we feel angry. But sometimes we do nothing even though we have just found new tools for making a positive difference. In the past, when we waited, it was not because we weren't people of action. We just hadn't known we could find good options. Now it's a new ballgame. An Anger Makeover provides good options.

Sometimes the reason we procrastinate and don't talk about anger and conflict may be that we're afraid of hurting the other person or stirring up trouble—and maybe rightly so. In fact, we need to keep in mind there are people who will feel hurt or think we are stirring up trouble no matter what we say. Some people do manipulate others, whether knowingly or unconsciously. No matter whether we blow up or remain silent, we will feed into their habit. In such cases it is even more essential that we take time to do an Anger Makeover—for ourselves, for the sake of our inner peace, and for our own integrity. Several things change when we simply use it to think through the conflict.

1. Our brain gets clearer, with more practical, positive ideas.
2. Our feelings change from cringing to confidence.
3. We know what we believe in and what we want.

It lets us stop fumbling around looking for the sense and non-sense in what the loved one said or did.

If Your Action Plan Takes Shape Spontaneously, Let It.

Often, by the time you get through the first four steps, a plan is already emerging, thanks to the options you discover. You may know exactly how you want to manage your irritation with the other person. It might be just, "Can we find a time to talk about this?" That's what Sister Helen (pp. 127-128, 138, and 142-143) decided she wanted to do with the Sister who went on strike and stopped chanting whenever she was disgusted with the community's prayer-time chanting. And Ana Maria (pp. 60-75 and 138) got to the heart of the matter. She simply let her husband know in plain English how important independent thought is for her, and how distressed she was with his dependent behaviors. The Anger Makeover helped these people take up their own banner proudly, stop doubting themselves, and not slip into frustration or bickering.

Accept the Creative Challenge

So, once you have done an Anger Makeover, whether in your head, on paper, or with another person's help, you are ready to do something with the relationship problem you selected to work on—but only if taking action makes sense.

I don't give out many rules for handling this. I'm me, and you're you. Leave your creative doors open as you envision your plan. It may not be clear at first, but after exploring with the five steps, your plan is no longer just "let's see what happens." You have a new sense of yourself and your territory. You've already made a major change: You went forward with self-respect and vision instead of frustration and confusion. Now it's you who are the framework for creating your plan.

This book's guidelines for thinking and writing about the five Anger-Makeover steps serve you well in this direct contact phase: You can see what's happening and stick to the person's behavior instead of guessing at bad intent. You can experience your rich bag of feelings about it, so as not to blow up or judge the person. You can be clear about what you want, and share your beliefs. You can talk more gently about your vision, or clarify your friend's or loved one's vision of what's happening, or discuss what is possible.

Stay Loose: Hang On to Your Sense of Humor

Even if you don't think you are a creative person, you can try doing fun things in a conflict. Almost anyone can come up with ways to introduce humor and still avoid making light of serious concerns. Who knows what ideas may come to you? Here are some examples.

One elderly lady imagined a paper hat on her opponent's head to remind her that he was still a little boy inside.

Harold, a gas company executive, mentally put fuzzy ear muffs on his graying boss. The picture reminded him to smile inwardly, and he could speak clearly and distinctly when things got difficult.

One couple said they would ask each other, "How can we pen up the dogs of war long enough to talk?" It helped them get started. Even their discussion about their rules of engagement had a touch of fun in it.

Communication Still Frozen?
Stay Patient and Awake, Ready for the Thaw

What about times when we don't know what to do or say, or just aren't yet able to get ourselves to bring up peaceful tools to replace warlike mental weapons? It certainly has happened to me. I forget to do the Anger Makeover. Even when I have worked on an issue using the process, I sometimes feel as though both the friend I am irked with and I are in such different camps that communication is impossible. Sometimes that may be true, at least for a while.

Marital skirmishes can build, until couples find themselves spending thousands of dollars on lawyers. They even end up forbidden to talk to each other directly at all. All messages go through the lawyers. But when you're out of contact with someone, you *can* certainly still use an Anger Makeover to clarify for yourself what you want and value. That's what it's for. That by itself is a goal worth achieving. In addition, once you achieve that clarity, you're ready for a conversation, just in case. Who knows, a thaw may come, and you'll be ready with your requests, information, and especially better composure. If necessary, you might say, "Looks like we're at an impasse here. Would you like to get together after we've both had time to think?" And you can plug in a specific time to address it. Meanwhile, you'll feel clear about where you stand, instead of worrying about someone else's feelings, position, or problems. Hmm, I remember times I wish I had followed this good advice and geared up with an Anger Makeover just in case.

Talk with a Friend or Colleague About Your Plan

For many of us, a lot of this will naturally be new territory. Why do we expect ourselves to know exactly what to do right away? A counselor or friend can serve as a sounding board or guide.

Role Play What You Want to Say

Practicing what you want to say before you say it, or role playing it with a colleague can make all the difference. "Sometimes in my job I had to fire someone," said a former head of surgery in a teaching hospital. "I hated that worse than anything."

"What did you do?" I asked.

"After I learned about role play, it always went well. I felt prepared, once I had talked over what I was going to say ahead of time, or even role played it." With a grin, he added, "Once I got in the room, I usually didn't say anything I had planned to say—but I still felt prepared, and the conversation always went all right."

A Shift: from "Overly Reserved" to "Gently Honest"

Imagine what a gift it could be: giving feedback, clarity, and respect. When people who tend to be overly reserved start speaking up, it is a relief to their more-talkative friends. Or people who are in their element with rapid-fire talk may sometimes feel more comfortable with someone more like themselves—and that could be you or me, learning to be more comfortable with our verbal and outgoing side. It can be painful and scary for them if they have to guess what we're thinking, especially when we seem unhappy about something. I'm in favor of giving them a break from that pain by being a little more outgoing, more generous, like them. In this book I support more-equal two-way feedback, offered sooner.

I'm not suggesting that we argue and add to the confusion. Being argumentative would be a sad substitute for what we may be good at—respect and clear thinking. We may have gifts for shining a light on confusion. That could go a long way toward changing the world. Doing an Anger Makeover always helps me give clearer feedback. By making the methods outlined in this book our own, we get better skills for articulating the mistakes we see; letting people know our feelings; asking for what we want; defining our values and essential character; and thinking about better ways to respond. When you're ready, take the time to start sharing the benefits in your unique perspective.

Be Patient—and Persistent

Patiently help people adjust to your new style. My friend and colleague Strong Paulson reminded me to explain that any change you try will disturb your surroundings. When you start speaking up for yourself you may often meet with pushback from the system—others attempting to restore the familiar equilibrium. They have become resigned to the old interaction pattern. They may try to force it back into place.

Your coworker or spouse may think, "Wait a minute. This is not the response I'm used to." Friends may feel hurt, frustrated— or get stubborn. You may detect resistance to the change. You yourself may feel strange for a while.

Stick with it. Don't be surprised or discouraged. After learning to use the Anger-Makeover process, you probably won't want to limit yourself to your old, silent ways, so just patiently push forward.

"Nobody likes me anymore," groaned Steve, a 21-year-old manager at a burger chain, after learning the Anger-Makeover method and commencing to speak up for himself better. "Everyone thinks I'm turning into a jerk."

"It doesn't sound like you're being a jerk," I countered. I had already checked in with him. He was still treating the others with respect, not being offensive. Judging from his account, he was asking for the specific, competent work he wanted from employees, and he was asking in a responsible way. "Your workers' complaints can be a sign of progress," I said. "You're changing, and now they'll have to change too." I encouraged him to stay the course, and he went out relieved. When he realized that the resistance of employees was the natural result of his progress, he was ready to stick with the changes.

We need to stick with our newfound strengths and confidence, because the people around us automatically assume we're the same as we always were. Naturally they try to stuff us back in the box they are used to seeing us in. It takes a while for them to realize that our growing clarity and honesty are a gift to them. We've been in that old box for so long that our changes normally require adjustment from all concerned. As you change, not only you, but also your spouse, boss, or children may be doing cartwheels. Still, everyone will have to learn to deal with a different you—and a different kind of relationship. You can play a part in helping with the adjustment. Instead of being hurt or angry, just expect the resistance and find ways to help everyone ride out the period of readjustment.

I have been speaking to those of us who are making better use of our neglected expressive skills. An already expressive friend gave another helpful suggestion for those of us practicing more-reserved skills.

> Those of us who have been too expressive may also find that others have a hard time adjusting to a new approach from us. Many times, people are glad we've slowed down, but others who are accustomed to an unequal relationship may be puzzled or mistrustful. This readjustment also takes time to settle in. If we are on good terms with the other person, we can even give them permission to help us hold our horses some and let them talk more, to make a better, more-equal conversation.

Coach People in How to Relate to the New You

You're not going to be changing in a vacuum. When you change, your environment must change too. Your colleagues, friends, and family will probably need help in making the adjustment. So, besides changing your style, you may need to give an additional gift: teaching them how to support you in your changes. And remember, you may have to keep after them while they learn to do these things.

There are three things you can ask of overly expressive friends (or of yourself, if you are overly expressive with them):

1. Keep insisting that they ask you what you think. And thank them when they do. If they impatiently try to read

your mind or tell you what you feel, or finish your sentences for you, point it out. You're no longer letting other people define you—or making them define you by not defining yourself.

2. You may have to keep patiently encouraging them to wait a second for you to say what you have to say. Let them know it will still sometimes take you a little time to figure out what you feel and think—and then how to put it into words. You can ask them to stay with the silence, and not give up on you when you're still pondering. Otherwise they automatically will think it's their turn and just start right in talking. Be ready to say, "Please wait a second. I'm not finished." Make sure they let you finish without interruption, even during your puzzled pauses.

"You have really helped me," said Amanda to her husband Earl, tapping her index finger on his shoulder, "by letting me know when you're not finished with what you're saying." She wouldn't have dreamed he was still thinking. She had always thought he had trailed off and dropped the subject. "Now I keep reminding myself to wait for you," she added. "And I like hearing your ideas."

If this is hard for you to keep doing, patiently reassure yourself too. The gifts that you've been withholding for so long are worth the wait.

3. Ask your friends to work out the solution along with you rather than impose their pat answer. We know people can be a little too sure they're right. Be persistent about interrupting that.

Even if you're timid, interrupt. But not if you're like my friend Pat: He always thinks he's right, because he usually is. He was highly offended when he realized I was advising someone to learn to interrupt. It was someone very different from him and in a very different situation. He told me, "No! Never interrupt." I was baffled but later saw that he was right—yet again—in his case. "Never" was the exactly right advice for Pat with his wife, who was weary of his constant interrupting. I figured out that his wife had had to make "never" the absolute rule for him after he had finally, for the billionth time, interrupted her once too often. She had clearly gotten her rule to stick for him, God bless her.

For you, the overly meek: Get your word in, edgewise if necessary. "Embrace your values" is not just a figure of speech. It means cherishing your wisdom. It means trusting your practical input. It means being a regular part of the problem-solving. It means recognizing what you know; revering what you believe in; and yes, being grateful for who you are.

This adjustment has two parts: working with yourself and working with the people around you. If you're in a situation where you are overly reserved and not getting equal time with a too-talkative partner,

1. For your part, you may need to learn to

    • Be impatient with their pushiness.
    • Ask them to wait and listen more.
    • Trust your insights.
    • Have the courage to speak up.

2. In exchange, they may need to learn, with your help, to

    • Be patient with your slower pace.
    • Interrupt you less.
    • Trust your insights.
    • Have the courage to listen and be receptive.

Again, my very-expressive friend reminded me, "For the expressive types, just switch roles to 'they may need to ...' in part 1. And 'I may need to ...' in part 2."

So, here's how that looks for you overly expressive folks not giving equal time to your too-quiet partner:

1. They (the other, quieter one) may need to learn to

    - Be impatient with your pushiness.
    - Ask you to wait and listen more.
    - Trust their insights.
    - Have the courage to speak up.

2. You may need to learn, with their help, to

    - Be patient with their slower pace.
    - Interrupt them less.
    - Trust their insights.
    - Have the courage to listen and be receptive.

If it's hard medicine for you, on either side, hang in there. We all get set in our ways. Life is change—not just for you, but for the system you are part of. Eventually, they will like the changes, and so will you.

It might be a good idea to get a copy of this book and give it to a significant other, so you both understand what you're dealing with. It could help you work together to develop new ways to interact.

A Final Reminder

So where from here? There are more ways to express ourselves than we can imagine. Just picturing effective ways starts to replace stale, hurtful ways. It's in your hands now. Will you step into a new future? You can use the Anger-Makeover process to bring heartfelt strength to yourself and your issues, one by one, instead of avoiding them. You can create a better past, present, and future. If you repair even one scenario, it lifts the heart, whether it's in the real world or still just in your imagination. You can pause long enough in conflicts to open the door for yourself to do your part, to work toward joint agreements—in imagery first, and then perhaps in reality. You can develop your tools and mental muscles. You can copy the worksheet on pages 56 and 57 and over and over use the Anger-Makeover process. You have what it takes to get real change going in your world, starting in your own backyard.

You start by transforming your own angers, irritations, and reactions into personal power.

Imagine moving on to include more makeovers besides the Anger Makeover. You can also reshape other instinctual and emotional reactions to enjoy a a powerful positive experience of your best Self. For example, this process works beautifully with fear too. People young and old can do a **Fear Makeover**, transforming their fear into a surprise grasp of their unique inner powers. Using these five-steps, can also do

a **Worry** Makeover

a **Too Honest** Makeover

an **Uncaring** Makeover

an **Unchecked Impulse** Makeover

a **Misery** Makeover

an **ADHD** Makeover

a **Depression** Makeover

a **Profanity** Makeover

a **Hopelessness** Makeover

an **Addiction** Makeover

a **Timidity** Makeover

a **Helplessness** Makeover

a **Bashfulness** Makeover

an **Avoidance** Makeover

a **Dead-in-the-Water** Makeover

a **What Isn't Working for You** Makeover.

Remember, the **P-O-W-E-R** steps work for you with all kinds of knee-jerk reactions.

P Picture the problem

O Own your emotions, in your body and emotions

W Want what you want—be specific

E Enjoy and embrace your values

R Review your range of options

APPENDIX

Conflict Skills Self-Check

Kind Expressiveness *and* Reserve

Here is a tool for pinpointing situations where an Anger Make-over would work well—and for deciding about how you want to express or not express the results you got.

It's for checking the expressive and reserved skills you tend to use in various conflict situations. Prepare for surprises.

**So, Okay, You've Used the Anger-Makeover Process.
Now I Invite You to Think About These Questions:**

1. Should I speak up more in this situation, or pull back?
2. What specific tools will make me more effective with this person (my boss, my children, etc.)?
3. What does the Anger-Makeover process offer me here and now?

First you can make a few copies of the self-check below, then use one each with various people and situations to adjust how you use your options.

Finish the First Three Sections, and Then Ask Yourself,

1. What did I learn?
2. What do I want to do differently with this person—for example, emphasize certain skills or de-emphasize certain weapons.
3. What next steps do I see—and am I willing to try them out mentally before I respond?

1. Pick One Situation or Person Where You Feel Irritation and Frustration.

Specifics about this person:

a coworker   *a boss...*

a family member _____

a child   *son*   *daughter*

yourself when you were younger

an acquaintance   *a stranger*

a friend   *a former friend*

a customer   _____

an institution/agency _____

God   _____

OTHER _____

Notes: _____

_____

_____

Other pressures you're feeling:

hungry

sick

in pain

in an anxious period

in a grief/loss/hurt period

busy, overworked

with observers present

OTHER pressures _____

_____

2. Recalling This Situation, Rate Your Conflict Skills in *Pairs* Below.

Circle "usually," "often," "sometimes," *or* "seldom,"
ON BOTH LEFT AND RIGHT SIDES OF THE PAGE.
Complete EACH LINE Before Going Down to the Next.

Stay loose; keep moving; guesses are okay.
(It's just for your eyes to see.)

In this situation, when I'm angry, scared, or hurt, I . . .

(Expressive Skills)	(Reserved Skills)
1. . . . push for what I want *usually often sometimes seldom*	. . . try not to be a bother *seldom sometimes often usually*
2. . . . show that I'm angry *usually often sometimes seldom*	. . . show that I'm scared or hurt *seldom sometimes often usually*
3. . . . jump into confrontation. *usually often sometimes seldom*	. . . put off confrontation *seldom sometimes often usually*
4. . . . am opinionated *usually often sometimes seldom*	. . . am accepting *seldom sometimes often usually*
5. . . . stand up for my rights *usually often sometimes seldom*	. . . stand up for the other's rights *seldom sometimes often usually*
6. . . . emphasize my importance *usually often sometimes seldom*	emphasize the other's importance *seldom sometimes often usually*
7. . . . am direct *usually often sometimes seldom*	. . . am indirect *seldom sometimes often usually*
8. . . . respond fast u*sually often sometimes seldom*	. . . respond slow *seldom sometimes often usually*
9. . . . push my ideas *usually often sometimes seldom*	. . . wait for the other person *seldom sometimes often usually*
10. . . . take charge *usually often sometimes seldom*	. . . back off *seldom sometimes often usually*

11. ... am sure of myself
usually often sometimes seldom

... question myself
seldom sometimes often usually

12. ... talk
usually often sometimes seldom

... listen
seldom sometimes often usually

13. ... have to be honest
usually often sometimes seldom

... seek the other's truth
seldom sometimes often usually

14. ... am outspoken
usually often sometimes seldom

... am quiet and withdrawn
seldom sometimes often usually

15. ... show impatience
usually often sometimes seldom

... show patience
seldom sometimes often usually

16. ... act impulsively
usually often sometimes seldom

... become thoughtful
seldom sometimes often usually

17. ... ignore my weak points
usually often sometimes seldom

... ignore the other's weak points
seldom sometimes often usually

18 .. point out the other's weak points
usually often sometimes seldom

... point out my weak points
seldom sometimes often usually

19. ... see my side
usually often sometimes seldom

... see the other person's side
seldom sometimes often usually

20. ... make my point
usually often sometimes seldom

... take in the other's point
seldom sometimes often usually

21. ... say what comes into my head
usually often sometimes seldom

... control what I say
seldom sometimes often usually

22. ... go for resolution
usually often sometimes seldom

... leave things open-ended
seldom sometimes often usually

23. ... pin down meanings
usually often sometimes seldom

... leave things ambiguous
seldom sometimes often usually

24. ... tend to be blunt
usually often sometimes seldom

... tend to be diplomatic
seldom sometimes often usually

25. ... point out my strengths
usually often sometimes seldom

... point out the other's strengths
seldom sometimes often usually

26. ... ignore the other's strengths
usually often sometimes seldom

... ignore my strengths
seldom sometimes often usually

27. . . . respect my interests.
usually often sometimes seldom

. . . respect the other's interests
seldom sometimes often usually

28. . . . focus on the other's mistakes
usually often sometimes seldom

. . . focus on my own mistakes
seldom sometimes often usually

29. . . . express myself
usually often sometimes seldom

. . . get the other to talk
seldom sometimes often usually

30. . . . focus on my position
usually often sometimes seldom

. . . focus on the other's position
seldom sometimes often usually

31. . . . try to please myself
usually often sometimes seldom

. . . try to please the other person
seldom sometimes often usually

32. . . . talk first
usually often sometimes seldom

. . . let the other person talk first
seldom sometimes often usually

33. . . . think, "I can't take this,"
and speak up
usually often sometimes seldom

. . . think, "no big deal," and let it go
seldom sometimes often usually

3. **How Much I Emphasize My Expressive Side, and How Much My Reserved Side:**

Now, for each side:

> *1. Record response counts,*
> *2. Multiply,*
> *3. Add the multiplied columns.*

> ### Expressive Response
>
> | | Count: | | Multiplied |
> |---|---|---|---|
> | *Usually* | _____ | *x 4 =* | _____ |
> | *Often* | _____ | *x 3 =* | _____ |
> | *Seldom* | _____ | *x 2 =* | _____ |
> | *Sometimes* | _____ | *x 1 =* | _____ |
>
> ### Reserved Response
>
> | | Count: | | Multiplied |
> |---|---|---|---|
> | *Usually* | _____ | *x 4 =* | _____ |
> | *Often* | _____ | *x 3 =* | _____ |
> | *Seldom* | _____ | *x 2 =* | _____ |
> | *Sometimes* | _____ | *x 1 =* | _____ |

Your Total Expressive Score: _____

Your Total Reserved Score: _____

Your scores in this situation may represent valuable qualities:

Expressive	Reserved
Self Care	Care for the Other
Self Protection	Protection for the Other
Self Expression	Respect, Receptiveness

- **Strengths**: Notice what skills you use with this person.

- **New Growth**: See whether the side you *give less emphasis to* can be your growing edge with this person. Notice where you circled "seldom." Which of these will be key skills to start developing first to explore any new growth, new emphasis, or changes to this relationship system? (Examples: If you circled seldom under item 27, "respect my interests," or item 32, "talk first," etc., these might be the key skills you want to start developing first.)

- **Different skills for different issues, people, situations**: For contrast, if you want to see how differently you interact in another conflict situation, you can pause here and do another self-check on another person and issue. You may want to highlight opposite strengths—and opportunities for growth—you didn't realize were available to you on both your expressive and reserved sides.

- **Synthesis of Opposites**: You can pull together strengths from both sides. Imagine emphasizing desired skills in a way that honors yourself and the other person. Here's a way you can begin experimenting:

List Pairs of Opposite Skills You'd Like to Combine When Dealing With This Issue:

1._____

2._____

3._____

4._____

Go on to the "weapons" section below. It underlines the importance of developing a synthesis of honoring yourself and the other person at the same time.

4. Harsh Weapons Awareness

Rate Your Use of Active-Aggressive Weapons and of Passive-Aggressive Weapons, as You Think of the Situation and Person You've Chosen for Your Focus.

When I'm angry, startled, or hurt, I...

| 1. ...fight | ...flee, freeze, or fawn |
| *usually often sometimes seldom* | *seldom sometimes often usually* |

| 2. ...use profanity | ...ignore the issue |
| *usually often sometimes seldom* | *seldom sometimes often usually* |

| 3. ...put the other person down | ...put myself down |
| *usually often sometimes seldom* | *seldom sometimes often usually* |

| 4. ...rule | ...comply and obey |
| *usually often sometimes seldom* | *seldom sometimes often usually* |

| 5. ...openly try to win | ...win sneakily |
| *usually often sometimes seldom* | *seldom sometimes often usually* |

| 6. ...get visible revenge | ...get underhanded revenge |
| *usually often sometimes seldom* | *seldom sometimes often usually* |

| 7. ...punish the other | ...punish myself |
| *usually often sometimes seldom* | *seldom sometimes often usually* |

| 8. ...scold, criticize | ...give the silent treatment |
| *usually often sometimes seldom* | *seldom sometimes often usually* |

Notice Possible Damages: Where you circled "often" and "usually," does it amount to mistreating yourself or the other person—and is it with aggression, or passiveness, or both?

Harmlessness: Consider replacing aggressive or passive-aggressive habits with skills honoring self and others. Look for skills at your growing edge, in the first part of the self-check, especially ones you want to experience more and keep developing.

A New Dawn: Give yourself a pat on the back for waking up to habits in this section that may be harming you or someone else.

Freedom: Congratulate yourself each time you reduce or eliminate a harmful habit in your daily life.

Note: I recommend having a professional help you with the changes you wish to make.

The objective is for you not just to be strong, but also reverent, and shrewd in how you choose your response to a friend or loved one. Our interactions can pave the way and help the world to find its way back to Self in conflicts. A choice is an act of will. Assagioli said people need to employ not just strong will, but also good will and skillful will. Our world desperately needs to interact with respect, reverence, and love.

Learning from the Self-Check and Changing Daily Life Conflict Practices

Did I pass or fail?

You can't fail this. It is not a test, it's a learning vehicle. It can show you how to improve your interactions with friends and loved ones. You may also see where you might want to use an Anger Makeover. (That may include conflicts where you have in the past leaned toward taking good care of the friend or loved one, but not yourself.)

How can boosting conflict skills on both my expressive and my reserved sides be good?

Both sides, expressive and reserved, represent skills that may be useful in the situation you chose. If the expressive side (left in the worksheet) is lower with this person, your expressive or anger energy may not be as available to you, and you may need to develop skills in self-care. If the reserved side (right in the worksheet) is lower, your reserved skills of energy, praise, and respect for others may not always be as available to you, and you may need to develop skills in caring for others. If you bolster your self-care and care of others, everybody wins.

What can I learn from this self-check?

1. **Observe a conflict style you use.** Each time you use the self-check, you see another variation of your conflict style with another person. You can learn which side of you is stronger in different situations. Either way, the Anger-Makeover process is made for you.

2. **Try out changes to your conflict styles.** Look especially for specific skills you may want to expand. Consider developing skills you haven't been using—while at the same time still supporting, even enhancing, opposite skills you find it easier to use. Suppose in a given situation you want to be more caring toward yourself. This doesn't mean you need to be less caring toward the other person. And suppose you decide you need to be more respectful, gentle, receptive to the other person. This doesn't mean you have to ignore your needs and wants. Notice especially which side of yourself you're neglecting and pick an appropriate skill to boost on that side. Gently find ways to increase use of that skill from **seldom** to **sometimes** (or to **often** or even **usually**).

3. **Become a flexible, variable synthesis of both sides of yourself.** Your mission, should you choose to accept it, is to become a synthesis of both expressiveness and reserve, and

in different ways depending on the situation—in other words, a powerful *and* loving person in various ways that suit who you are, wherever you are.

An example: Jill noticed that she was almost always letting her mother lead off when they had disagreements. After a self-check, she decided, "I'll try being first to talk, at least half the time." But what to say? She used an Anger Makeover to help her think clearly about the issues. That gave her a variety of appropriate, purposeful things to say, making it easier to speak up for herself more quickly and competently. Here's a way she might approach any such discussion. "Mom, I might like to discuss this with you. Do you think that would be okay, provided we can split the talk time 50-50 and agree on being kind to each other and on what we want to accomplish?"

Here's a tip on changing your conflict style. Say you're wanting to boost your self-care side. Try keeping track of your progress for two weeks and see what changes start to occur. Don't give up just because someone is put off by your new style. That could be a sign of progress. You could sit down with the person and have a little talk about what you're trying to accomplish, spelling out what you're doing differently and why it's important to you personally.

Take caution: With colleagues in some settings, especially in the highly competitive corporate world, the suggestion above, to talk about what you're trying to accomplish, may work against you. I heard the following from a high-level employee of a major American company.

> To think corporate America is a safe space is naïve. I have tried this maybe a couple of times—in small ways, because the risk is high that at work you could reinforce a reputation for your bad habits, or inform those who were not aware of them. That has real consequences that follow you. Arguably, the method can help. Some could be impressed by one's efforts.

But in the corporate setting, if one doesn't succeed—say a person trying to stop smoking or lose weight or stay sober—it seems like talking about what you're trying to accomplish can just add to a reputation.

You need to be clear that the person or group you're sharing your efforts with is safe.

Use of the Harsh Weapons Awareness Section

In the Weapons Awareness, harsh anger items may reveal ways you're likely to react that might be harmful. By looking at either kind of weapon (aggressive or passive) you see ways we may go overboard into aggression with our self-caring, or go into passive aggression with our other-caring.

Reducing hurtful habits can boost our effectiveness as boss, friend, employee, spouse, family member, or teammate. If you marked items **often** or **usually**, challenge yourself to reduce those items to **seldom** or **almost never**.

Increasing your effective, harmless habits makes it easier to *reduce* counterproductive, hurtful habits. That's where the Anger Makeover comes in handy: Habits that tie kindness and anger together will change you and your world.

Self-Check Summary

In sum, you can use the self-check for three things:

1. Getting a better grip on your interaction style in a given situation. Are you more expressive, or are you more reserved? And could an Anger-Makeover session help you get better results?
2. Polishing skills you're not using, anything from speaking up quickly to waiting and listening.
3. Reducing inappropriate or hurtful habits in your everyday world, finding specific ways to protect yourself as well as your friend or loved one.

Notes:

[1] https://allpoetry.com/Last-Night-As-I-Was-Sleeping, Translated by Robert Bly
[2] www.undefendedheart.org
[3] https://allpoetry.com/poem/8534703-The-Guest-House-by-Mewlana-Jalaluddin-Rumi

SELECTED RESOURCES

Adams, L. with Lenz, E. (1979). *Effectiveness Training for Women.* New York: Perigee Books.

Assagioli, R. (1999). *The Act of Will.* Woking, England: David Platts Publishing Company.

Assagioli, R. (1976). *Psychosynthesis.* New York: Penguin.

Bach, G.R., & Goldberg, H. (1974). *Creative Aggression.* Garden City, N.Y.: Doubleday.

Bramson, R. (1992). *Coping with Difficult Bosses.* New York: Simon and Schuster.

Bramson, R. (1989). *Coping with Difficult People.* New York: Simon and Schuster.

Brown, M.Y. (1993). *Growing Whole.* New York: Hazelden (Harper Collins).

Brown, M.Y. (2009). *Growing Whole: Self-Realization for the Great Turning.* Mt Shasta, CA: Psychosynthesis Press.

Brown, M.Y. (1983). *The Unfolding Self: Psychosynthesis and Counseling.* Los Angeles: Psychosynthesis Press.

Bums, D. (1973). *Feeling Good.* New York: Basic Books (Harper Colophon).

Carter, J. J, (1989). *Nasty People: How to Stop Being Hurt by Them Without Becoming One of Them.* Chicago: Contemporary Books.

DiGiuseppe, R. (1997). *Assessment, Diagnosis and Treatment of Clients with Anger Problems.* Workshop through David R. Lima, ACSW, Inc. Mentor, Ohio 44060.

Evans, P. (1992). *The Verbally Abusive Relationship: How to Recognize it and How to Respond.* Holbrook, MA: Bob Adams.

Fay, J. and Cline, F.W. (1996). *Avoiding Power Struggles with Kids.* Golden, CO.: The Love and Logic Press Inc.

Ferrucci, P. (2007). *The Power of Kindness: The Unexpected Bene-fits of Leading a Compassionate Life.* New York: Jeremy P. Tarcher/Penguin.

Ferrucci, P. (1982). *What We May Be.* Los Angeles: Tarcher.

Firman, J. & Vargiu, J. (1977). "Dimensions of Growth." *Synthesis 3-4,* 59-120.

Gordon, T. (1975). *Parent Effectiveness Training.* New York: Peter H. Wyden.

Haronian, F. (1967). *Repression of the Sublime.* Psychosynthesis Research Foundation.

Harris, P. (1989). *Music and Self: Living your Inner Sound.* Albuquerque, NM: Intermountain Publishing.

Lerner, H.G. (1985). *The Dance of Anger.* New York: Perennial Library (Harper and Row).

Maslow, A. H. (1993). *The Farther Reaches of Human Nature.* Big Sur, CA: Esalen.

Menakem, R. (2017). *My Grandmother's Hands: Racialized Trauma and the Pathway to Mending Our Hearts and Bodies.* Las Vegas, NV: Central Recovery Press.

Miller, A. (1983). *For Your Own Good: Hidden Cruelty in Child-Rearing and the Roots of Violence.* New York: Farrar, Strauss, and Giroux.

Piaget, G. & Binkley, B. (1984). *Dealing with Difficult People.* Washington, DC: American Psychological Assoc.

Polt, W. (1984). "From Anger to Power." *Psychosynthesis Digest, #IV Vol. II, No. 2.* 44-73.

Polt, W. (1996). *From Anger to Power: A Clear Thought & Straight Talk Method for Our Everyday World.* Albuquerque, NM: Intermountain Publishing.

Rosenberg, M. B. (1996). *Connecting Compassionately* (audio tape). The Center for Nonviolent Communication, 3229 Bordeaux St., Sherman, TX 95090.

Rosenberg, M. B. (2015). *Nonviolent Communication: A Language of Life: Life-Changing Tools for Healthy Relationships.* Encinitas, CA: PuddleDancer Press.

Rumi, J. (2004). *Selected Poems* (C. Barks with J.Moynce, A. J.Arberry, R. Nicholson, trans.). New York: Penguin Books.

Siegel, D. J. (2011). *Mindsight: The New Science of Personal Transformation.* New York: Bantam Books.

Skitka, L. J., Bauman, C. W., & Sargis, E.G. (2005). "Moral Conviction: Another Contributor to Attitude Strength or Something More?" *Journal of Personality and Social Psychology*, 88(6), 895-917.

Smith, B. V. "How and to what are you paying attention? And why does it matter?" Retrieved September 7, 2020 from https://www.undefendedheart.org/attention.html

Smith, B. V. (2019). "Inherent Synthesis of Human & Being." *Psychosynthesis Quarterly*, 7(5), 22-24.

Sonkin, D. J. & Durphy, M. (1982). *Learning to Live Without Violence: A Handbook for Men.* San Francisco: Volcano Press.

Stauffer, E. (1987). *Unconditional Love and Forgiveness.* Burbank: Triangle.

Tavris, C. (1983). *Anger, the Misunderstood Emotion.* New York: Simon and Schuster.

Thich Naht Hanh. (1996). *Teachings on Love* (audio tape). Sounds True Audio 735 Walnut St., Boulder, CO 80302 (800/333-9185).

Trafton, J. A., Gordon, W. P., & Misra, S. (2019). *Training Your Brain to Adopt Healthful Habits: Mastering the Five Brain Challenges* (3rd ed.). Los Altos, CA: Institute for Brain Potential.

Vargiu, J. (1974). "Subpersonalities." *Synthesis I*, 52-90.

Viljoen, E. (2017). *Ordinary Goodness: The Surprisingly Effortless Path to Creating a Life of Meaning and Beauty.* New York: Penguin Random House LLC.

Van Boven, L., Lowenstein, G., Dunning, D., Nordgren, L. (2013). *Changing Places: A Dual Judgment Model of Empathy Gaps in Emotional Perspective Taking* (PDF)

Weisinger, H.D. (1985). *Anger Work-Out Book.* New York: Quill.

Wiesel, E. (1986). Elie Wiesel foundation for humanity. Remember. https://eliewieselfoundation.org/elie-wiesel/nobelprizespeech/

INDEX

C

caring, 6, 17, 38, 43, 47-48, 63, 77-79, 82, 89, 109, 122, 129, 139-140, 151, 162, 190, 192

change, changing, xiii, xv, xvi, 5, 9, 12, 13, 17, 18, 23, 24, 27-28, 34, 38-40, 46, 48, 49, 51, 54-55, 60, 63, 70, 73, 75, 77, 79, 84, 85, 89, 97-99, 102-103, 112, 116-117, 120, 126-133, 145, 147, 153-155, 158, 160-161, 163-164, 167, 170-171, 173-175, 178, 179, 189, 191, 192, 197

clarity, 71, 131, 164, 169, 172-174

colleagues, ix, xii, 8, 16, 26, 27, 50-52, 86, 100, 102, 122, 146, 175, 191

communication, 35, 62, 104, 113, 139, 154-156, 158, 159, 172

compassion, 18, 82, 84, 88, 120, 136, 142-143, 157

compromise, 26, 167

confidence, 71, 72, 75, 93, 114, 115, 143, 169, 170, 174

conflicts, iii, ix-x, xii, xvii, 3, 16, 25, 28-29, 31, 32, 41, 42, 50, 55, 78, 93, 98, 103, 104, 107, 113, 152, 158, 161, 163-164, 168, 178, 189, 208

confrontation, 160, 183

conscience, 163-164

conscientious, 30, 109, 163

conscious, 32, 79, 85, 87, 88, 106, 152, 159

constructive, x, 24, 25, 32, 51, 52, 63, 83, 114, 116, 117, 128, 148, 151, 159, 166, 168

control, xvii, 3-5, 13, 21-22, 25, 34, 37, 39, 40, 44, 46, 64, 65, 86, 105, 110, 112, 117, 121, 127, 145, 184

conversation, 8, 42, 43, 154, 172, 173, 175

conviction, ix, 7, 26-27, 50, 138, 140, 155, 162, 196

cooperation, 62, 71, 101, 133, 135, 166, 167

couples, xvi, 8, 15, 16, 52, 164, 172

Couples Institute, 21

Creative Challenge, 170

criticism, 15, 16, 63, 65-67, 78

curious, x, 7

cycles, 7-8

D

Dalai Lama, xiv

daring, 119

deal, 20, 63, 86, 99, 100, 107, 115, 116, 130, 135, 166, 175, 185

Deal Making, 166

decisions, 18, 25, 31, 114, 127, 163, 164

default, 4, 7-8, 122

defense, xi, 62, 88, 146, 148, 168

depressed, 46, 111, 115, 142, 167

depression, 115, 179

differentiation, 13, 21, 51, 61, 161

dignity, 140, 145, 164-166

discipline, 79, 116

discourse, 146

R

A son of the American heartlands, **Walter Polt, MA, LCPC,** learned all too soon to be nice—and to hide anger. His book on anger in relationships gives five steps to turning your negative impulses positive and feeling clear and confident about your preferences and values—so you're ready to speak up with love and respect. After doing his graduate work in counseling at Columbia, he was licensed as a Masters Social Worker in New Mexico and is now a Licensed Clinical Professional Counselor. For more than four decades, he has counseled, coached, and presented international trainings in diverse settings including outpatient mental health, community mental health, and private practice. Psychosynthesis inspires him. It's a spacious growth-and-integration system founded by Robert Assagioli, MD. When Edith Stauffer, PhD, taught Walter her process of Unconditional Love and Forgiveness he rediscovered his anger and started putting it to good use. He followed his passion: guiding people to avoid anger's tricks and to train their brains in habits of compassion and cooperation. He cocreated Intermountain Associates for Psychosynthesis and its training program, has served on the Steering Committee of the Association for the Advancement of Psychosynthesis, and has written numerous professional articles.